teach yourself

linux

linux
robert billing

For over sixty years, more than
40 million people have learnt over
750 subjects the **teach yourself**
way, with impressive results.

be where you want to be
with **teach yourself**

For UK order enquiries: please contact Bookpoint Ltd, 130 Milton Park, Abingdon, Oxon OX14 4SB. Telephone: +44 (0) 1235 827720. Fax: +44 (0) 1235 400454. Lines are open 09.00–18.00, Monday to Saturday, with a 24-hour message answering service. Details about our titles and how to order are available at www.teachyourself.co.uk

For USA order enquiries: please contact McGraw-Hill Customer Services, PO Box 545, Blacklick, OH 43004-0545, USA. Telephone: 1-800-722-4726. Fax: 1-614-755-5645.

For Canada order enquiries: please contact McGraw-Hill Ryerson Ltd, 300 Water St, Whitby, Ontario L1N 9B6, Canada. Telephone: 905 430 5000. Fax: 905 430 5020.

Long renowned as the authoritative source for self-guided learning – with more than 40 million copies sold worldwide – the **teach yourself** series includes over 300 titles in the fields of languages, crafts, hobbies, business, computing and education.

British Library Cataloguing in Publication Data: a catalogue record for this title is available from the British Library.

Library of Congress Catalog Card Number: on file.

First published in UK 2004 by Hodder Education, 338 Euston Road, London, NW1 3BH.

First published in US 2004 by Contemporary Books, a Division of the McGraw-Hill Companies, 1 Prudential Plaza, 130 East Randolph Street, Chicago, IL 60601 USA.

This edition published 2005.

The **teach yourself** name is a registered trade mark of Hodder Headline.

Copyright © 2004 Robert Billing

In UK: All rights reserved. Apart from any permitted use under UK copyright law, no part of this publication may be reproduced or transmitted in any form or by any means, electronic or mechanical, including photocopy, recording, or any information, storage and retrieval system, without permission in writing from the publisher or under licence from the Copyright Licensing Agency Limited. Further details of such licences (for reprographic reproduction) may be obtained from the Copyright Licensing Agency Limited, of 90 Tottenham Court Road, London W1T 4LP.

In US: All rights reserved. Except as permitted under the United States Copyright Act of 1976, no part of this publication may be reproduced or distributed in any form or by any means, or stored in a database or retrieval system, without the prior written permission of Contemporary Books.

Typeset by Servis Filmsetting Ltd, Manchester.
Printed in Great Britain for Hodder Education, a division of Hodder Headline, 338 Euston Road, London NW1 3BH, by Cox & Wyman Ltd, Reading, Berkshire.

Hodder Headline's policy is to use papers that are natural, renewable and recyclable products and made from wood grown in sustainable forests. The logging and manufacturing processes are expected to conform to the environmental regulations of the country of origin.

Impression number   10 9 8 6 5 4 3

Year   2010 2009 2008 2007 2006 2005

contents

	acknowledgements	viii
01	**getting started with linux**	**1**
	1.1 introduction	2
	1.2 background	3
	1.3 Linux distributions	6
	1.4 how and where to obtain a distribution	7
	1.5 installing Linux	8
	1.6 installing a dual-boot system	12
	1.7 what to do if installation fails (*optional*)	12
	1.8 getting support	16
	1.9 Linux on laptops	17
02	**the alternatives**	**18**
	2.1 Debian	19
	2.2 SuSE	20
	2.3 Gentoo	21
	2.4 Knoppix	21
	2.5 non-Intel platforms	21
03	**using linux**	**23**
	3.1 types of data	24
	3.2 sessions and logging in	25
	3.3 the file tree and file paths	27
	3.4 the Command Language Interpreter (*optional*)	29
	3.5 filesystems	37

	3.6 the /proc filesystem	42
	3.7 special files	43
	3.8 X-Windows	43
	3.9 the Graphical User Interface (GUI)	49
04	**software that runs on linux**	**51**
	4.1 office applications	52
	4.2 graphical tools	63
	4.3 some other interesting applications	66
	4.4 games	71
	4.5 web, mail and news	71
05	**more powerful features**	**76**
	5.1 basic scripting (*optional*)	77
	5.2 using cron	81
	5.3 printing	84
	5.4 emulating other environments (*optional*)	89
06	**linux and networking**	**92**
	6.1 TCP/IP basics	93
	6.2 internet access	101
	6.3 troubleshooting TCP/IP	103
	6.4 file sharing	110
	6.5 using automount	112
	6.6 interworking with Microsoft systems	114
	6.7 interworking with classical UNIX	118
	6.8 interworking with other common systems	119
	6.9 telnet, rsh and ssh	119
07	**network management and servers**	**122**
	7.1 PPP	123
	7.2 PLIP	124
	7.3 Linux servers and clients	125
	7.4 network security	134
	7.5 network caching	140
08	**maintaining the system**	**142**
	8.1 installing, configuring and removing packages	143

	8.2	making backups	145
09	**inside linux**		**170**
	8.3	recovering from disasters	156
	8.4	common problems	167
09	**inside linux**		**170**
	9.1	the startup and shutdown sequences	171
	9.2	modules and drivers	179
10	**programming for beginners (*optional*)**		**183**
	10.1	basic development tools	184
	10.2	GUI applications and widget sets	187
	10.3	serial interface	187
	10.4	TCL, TK and `tix`	188
	10.5	Perl	193
11	**careers with linux**		**195**
	11.1	certification	196
	11.2	career development	197
12	**advanced topics (optional)**		**198**
	12.1	embedded linux	199
	12.2	real-time linux	200
	12.3	configuring and compiling the kernel	202
	12.4	creating packages	207
	taking it further		**212**
	glossary		**216**
	index		**223**

acknowledgements

To my late father, Bernard Billing, who taught me what the ones and zeroes meant.

Thanks to my wife, Kath Billing, for putting up with me through the long months that *Teach Yourself Linux* has taken to write, to the members of the Forward Motion writing community and Reading Writers' Group for their help and support and to Jenny Hewitt who showed me how to put a book together.

Particular thanks to Connor Caple, Richard Crook, Colin Fisk, Margaret Fisk, Simon Heywood, Neil Jarvis, Joshua Johnston, Jinx Kimmer, Holly Lisle, Mike Mendelsohn, Alan Morgan, Kenneth Norris, John Shepherd, Robert Sloan, Linda Sprinkle and Leon Ward for reading the book in manuscript and offering constructive comments.

Linux is a registered trademark of Linus Torvalds.

01
getting started with linux

In this chapter you will learn:

- how Linux was created
- what a distribution is and how to obtain one
- how to install both single and dual-boot systems
- how to deal with installation problems
- how to obtain support
- how to run Linux on a laptop

1.1 Introduction

Linux is an operating system that has proved itself highly effective on both servers and desktop computers. It is also finding its way into applications as diverse as video recorders, telecommunications systems and spacecraft.

This book will give you an introduction to Linux. It will show you how to set up and begin using a simple Linux system, and how to find the sources of information that will enable you to go on learning on your own.

Because some users only want to know enough to get a system working, and others are interested in what goes on inside Linux, I have marked some sections of this book with the word *optional*. These optional sections are also useful if you get into difficulties, particularly during the installation phase, and want to solve the problem yourself, rather than asking for help.

Linux, and open-source software in general, uses some new terminology. To make this more understandable I have placed each new term in italics *like this* the first time it occurs. A short glossary of terms and acronyms appears at the end of the book.

You will need a computer on which you are free to try things out. Any personal computer with a Pentium or similar processor, even a very old one, can be used. You will need as an absolute minimum 12 megabytes of *Random Access Memory* (RAM) and 2 gigabytes of disk space. That is an *absolute* minimum – Linux will only just run in a machine that small. To have Linux run reasonably quickly and with every feature working you will need 128 megabytes of RAM and 5 gigabytes of disk space.

Almost any graphics card, keyboard and mouse will do.

It is possible to work through the exercises using a computer which has another operating system installed on it. However if you want to experiment with the installation process – as I hope you will – there is a small but very real risk of erasing all the data on the hard disk. This causes no permanent damage to the machine but can be very inconvenient. If you choose this route it is very important that you make a backup of all your data before you begin installation.

The best plan is to obtain an old machine on which you can experiment safely. These can often be acquired very cheaply – you may even find a friend who has one to give away.

Ideally you will also need an internet connection. At the time of writing there are some internal modems that will not work with Linux. An external modem, or a connection to the internet via a Local Area Network (LAN) will almost certainly work at the first attempt.

1.2 Background

An operating system, such as Linux, is a collection of programs which carry out many routine tasks on a computer. It also provides a safe way in which application programs, such as games and word processors, can get access to screen, keyboard, mouse, printer and disk.

The largest part of the operating system, and the one on which all the others depend, is called the *kernel*. The kernel is started when the computer is switched on or reset.

Peripherals, such as the hard disk, respond to very simple commands. Applications, such as word processors, which are seen by the person sitting in front of the screen, expect to do complicated things. The kernel must mediate between them.

Click with the mouse on a word processor's file menu and select a file to open. The word processor will send a request to the kernel for the file. The kernel then works out where that file is on the hard disk. It issues a command to the hard disk to look in the correct place and read the right number of characters. These characters are then handed back, by the kernel, to the word processor and the file appears on the screen.

Because the kernel sees every request for access to the disk it can veto any that might do damage to the system. Linux makes a sharp distinction between files owned by the system itself and files owned by users. Similarly it can prohibit a user program from directly issuing commands to peripherals such as the disk drives.

If, for example, the person using the word processor tries to save their document in /etc, an area reserved by Linux for its own files, the kernel will simply turn the request away with an error message.

This sharp distinction between what someone using the system can do, and what is permitted to the system itself, constitutes most of Linux's resistance to attack. A malign program run by an ordinary user simply cannot make any changes to the operating system. Malicious attacks on Linux machines do still happen but they require a high degree of programming skill, often do little damage and are very easy to counter.

The terms *user* and *root* are used to describe the environments inhabited by ordinary users and by the operating system itself. *Root* and *root login* also refer to a person who has administrator privileges over a particular computer. When this person logs in they can do things that are forbidden to ordinary users.

The first version of the Linux kernel was written as a hobby project by Linus Torvalds in the early 1990s, working alone in a flat in Helsinki. When this was combined with Richard Stallman's supporting programs and Bob Scheifler's X-Windows graphical interface it became a complete system. Because of this it has been argued that the word Linux is really only applicable to the kernel itself, even though it is commonly used for the whole system.

The name Linux is a conflation of *Linus* and *UNIX*, an older operating system developed at Bell Laboratories in the late 1960s and early 1970s. Many features of Linux are based on the older UNIX system.

Linux is copyrighted. Its components are owned by their various authors. They are released under the terms of the *General Public Licence* or GPL, a document originated by the *Free Software Foundation* (FSF). This licence gives to anyone the right to use, copy and modify the software. Because of this it can be completely legal to buy one copy of a CD containing Linux, make a copy of the CD, then use the original to install Linux on several machines. At the same time you may sell the copy of the CD to someone else who then installs Linux on several of their machines.

The word Linux is a registered trademark of Linus Torvalds and should be acknowledged when used – as it is at the start of this book.

Patents have been applied for on some of the software techniques developed for Linux. However, the GPL has been effective in ensuring that the patented techniques are freely available to all users.

Figure 1.1 is a roadmap of a Linux system. As a map it is far from complete – one sheet of paper cannot hope to show the hundreds

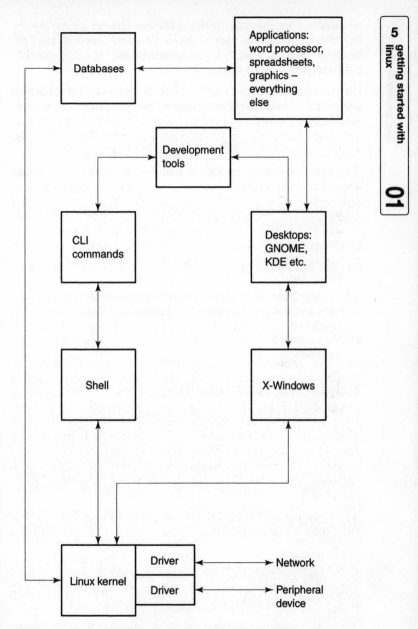

Figure 1.1 Linux roadmap (CLI is the abbreviation for Command Language Interpreter, explained in section 3.4)

of interlocking subsystems that you can run on Linux. At the bottom is the Linux kernel itself, and built into it are two modular drivers, one for the network and one for another peripheral, perhaps a disk.

On top of the kernel sits a shell and on top of that a wealth of commands. These can be used to drive the system by typing commands at the keyboard.

The X-Windows system also sits on top of the kernel. It provides the basic mechanisms for handling the display. You then have a choice of desktops and window managers which give the system a specific 'look and feel'.

The application programs then ride on the desktops, and make use of services such as databases and networking.

EXERCISES

1.1 Visit the website `http://www.linux.org` and follow some of the links.
1.2 Read the GPL at `http://www.fsf.org` and compare it with the licence on a conventional commercial software product.
1.3 If you know anyone who uses Linux, ask them about their experiences.

1.3 Linux distributions

A working Linux system consists of many hundreds, sometimes thousands, of files. A kit which contains all the files and some programs to copy them to their right places on the hard disk is called a *distribution*. Distributions can also include printed instruction books, registration cards, CDs of application programs and in some cases advertising material such as T-shirts and car stickers.

Distributions are manufactured by either commercial or voluntary organizations. Because the software in a distribution is released under the GPL it is always possible to obtain one almost free of charge.

If you would like to experiment with Linux before starting installation you can use the Knoppix distribution to bring up Linux from a CD-ROM without altering anything on your hard disk.

One of the most commonly used distributions is RedHat Linux, created by Red Hat Inc. of Raleigh, North Carolina, USA. In the interests of simplicity the worked examples will be shown for version 9.0 of this distribution, current at the time of writing. RedHat Linux is a commercial distribution. The same software is included in the free Fedora distribution, http://www.fedora.redhat.com. However almost everything in this book is equally applicable to SuSE, Debian, Yellow Dog and many other distributions. In time you will choose one or more distributions that suit your needs from the many that are available.

EXERCISE

1.4 Visit the websites of at least three distribution manufacturers. Most of these can be found by following links from http://www.linux.org. Compare their products and make a note of the version number of the most up-to-date version of each distribution.

1.4 How and where to obtain a distribution

All the major distributions can be downloaded free of charge from the internet. As a first-time user you will probably find this process daunting. My advice is to start off by buying a distribution on CD-ROM and only attempt to download distributions once you have some experience with using Linux on the internet.

You can buy a distribution in two ways. The distribution manufacturers supply 'boxed sets' which contain the software on CD-ROM, a printed manual and registration cards shrinkwrapped in a cardboard box. Alternatively a number of vendors offer 'cheap disks' which are in effect clones of the major distributors' disks at very low prices.

Because the provisions of the GPL explicitly forbid any restrictions on copying Linux the cheap disk versions are completely legitimate. However, to protect the considerable investment that some distribution manufacturers have put into their products we are seeing a spate of odd strategies designed to shepherd the users towards buying commercial boxed sets. These include trademarks, copyrighted images displayed when the computer is started and non-GPL software included on the disks.

In general, boxed sets are the easiest way for a first-time user to obtain a distribution. They may also include telephone and e-mail support as part of the package, which can be very useful initially. Cheap disk versions contain the same software but without the helpful installation guides or the support. They are a good way of buying further revisions of a distribution in order to upgrade running machines.

High street computer shops often stock the boxed sets and occasionally the cheap versions as well. However, it is worth checking the version numbers before buying, as slow turnovers can mean that versions over a year out of date are being offered for sale. These distributions work but do not have the most up-to-date revisions of the software.

More specialized shops, particularly if the staff are themselves Linux users, offer a better service.

Distributions can also be bought by mail, telephone or secure internet ordering. I have been very satisfied with the service I have received from *The Linux Emporium* of Swansea, http://www.linuxemporium.co.uk/. I hasten to add that I have no connection with this business, other than as a customer.

If you are in business in the UK and use Linux it is possible to reclaim input value added tax (VAT) on the software part of Linux distributions. The printed manuals do not carry VAT. Because of this it is important to check your receipt carefully as the VAT component of an order for both software and manuals may not be the expected fraction of the total invoice amount.

EXERCISE

1.5 Review the results of the previous exercise. Choose which distribution you would like to use and obtain a copy.

1.5 Installing Linux

The installation process varies greatly between distributions, and between revisions of the same distribution. Because of this it is impossible to give a step-by-step guide which is applicable in all cases. However, all installations have to do the same things and in this section I will explain in general terms how the installation process works and what each step does.

Before starting installation it is useful to find out exactly what hardware you have and how it is configured. If the computer you are using has another operating system already installed on it make a note of any information about the hardware you can glean from its setup pages. In particular make a note of the type, memory size and settings of the graphics card and the type and settings of the sound card.

The first step in the installation process is to load and run the Linux kernel. With many modern machines all you need to do is insert the first CD of the Linux distribution in the CD-ROM drive and start the computer. With older machines that cannot use the CD-ROM as the boot device you must first copy the kernel onto a floppy and use that to start the installation process.

You will find the rawrite program included in almost all distributions. This program copies enough of Linux onto a floppy disk from the CD to get the installation started. It is called rawrite because it writes to the raw disk, ignoring any file structure that is already on it. The installation instructions which came with your distribution will explain exactly how to use rawrite. Usually this involves copying an image file (a file that contains exactly the same data, formatted in the same way, as a floppy disk) from the CD to a floppy. Remember that this will erase everything on the floppy.

If you want to install Linux onto a computer that does not have a CD-ROM drive, but does have a network connection, the easiest way to do it is to use rawrite to make a network boot disk and then use this to start the installation process. You will also need to copy the installation CDs from your distribution onto another machine's hard drive; this will require up to 2 gigabytes of disk space. This copy of the CD is then shared to the network and used in place of a CD-ROM. Once again, if you have a distribution that allows you to do this, simply follow the instructions. It is possible to install Linux onto a machine that has neither a CD-ROM nor a network port. This involves loading the software through either the printer port or a serial connection. Before doing this you should read the sections on networking in later chapters, and ideally gain some experience of a more conventional system first.

Once the kernel is running on the target machine (the computer on which you are installing Linux), it will search the machine to see what hardware is available, then it will start the installation process itself.

The next step is *partitioning* the hard disk drive. It is convenient to store different kinds of information on different parts of the disk, called partitions. A Linux installation normally uses two or three partitions. These are the *root partition* which contains almost all of the ordinary files, the optional *boot partition* from which the kernel is loaded when the computer starts, and the *swap partition* which is used by Linux as temporary storage for tasks which are not doing anything at the moment. You only need a boot partition if you have an older computer which has to load the kernel from the first part of the hard disk.

The installation programs supplied with most distributions will divide the hard disk into partitions automatically for a simple installation, and will give you the option of leaving a previously installed operating system untouched. If the installation program cannot create the partitions automatically, or if you want to experiment with more complicated partitioning schemes, you can choose to partition the disk manually. The hard disk on the computer I am using to write this book is divided into fifteen partitions and has four different operating systems installed.

Once the hard disk has been partitioned the installation program will make *filesystems* within the partitions. This is roughly equivalent to taking a blank sheet of paper and ruling lines on it to turn it into a form, making it ready to have information written on it.

The installation program will, somewhere around this stage, pause and ask you what optional software you want to install. The first time you perform an installation it is probably best to accept the installation program's advice and select whatever it thinks is a normal or default system.

The longest part of the installation comes next. The installation program will copy all the files containing the Linux system onto the hard disk. This can take anything between ten minutes and several hours depending on the amount of software to be installed and the speed of the hardware.

Once the software is in place the installation program will attempt to find out what sort of graphics card is installed in your computer and what sort of monitor you have. With modern hardware this process is often completely automatic. With an older machine it is sometimes necessary to tell the installation program what hardware you have.

Monitors are quite easy to identify – they usually have a maker's name and model number printed on them somewhere, often underneath or at the back. Graphics cards can be more troublesome. The best way of identifying one is to find the original handbook that came with the card. If the computer was already working – with another operating system – when you first obtained it you may be able to find the details of the card within that system's settings. It is also sometimes possible to identify a graphics card by looking in the /proc filesystem, this is described in Chapter 3. If all else fails the only solution may be to remove the card from the machine and look for the maker's name and model number.

Once the graphics card and monitor have been identified the installation program will try out the maximum display resolution that it thinks is possible with that combination.

If this produces a satisfactory display you can safely proceed to the next step of the installation. If not, you may have to experiment with the settings.

The setup program may give you a choice of a graphical or text login. Only select the graphical login if you are completely satisfied that the previous step has correctly set up your graphics card and monitor.

Finally the installation program will ask you how to set up the *boot loader*. This is a little program which loads the Linux kernel into memory and starts it when your computer is reset. The default setting – to install the boot loader at the beginning of the hard disk – is normally the correct one.

If the installation offers you the opportunity to create an emergency boot disk, also known as a recovery disk, accept it. Label this disk and put it in a safe place. It will enable you to restart the machine if the boot loader is damaged.

At some point the installation program will ask you to set the root password. This password must be quoted correctly to log in as root once the system is running. Choose a word or phrase which is not obvious. Your name, the names of your friends and family, pets and makes of car are too easily guessed. Opening a book at random and putting your finger on a word is safer, choosing two words and a number at random, giving a password such as working52expire is much more secure.

You may also have the opportunity at this stage to add one or more users. Include everyone who will be using the system, giving them all distinct passwords, chosen as above. User logins will be explained in Chapter 3.

If everything has gone correctly you will now have a working Linux system. If not, section 1.7 will explain some useful strategies for recovering from an installation failure.

EXERCISE

1.6 Install your chosen distribution.

1.6 Installing a dual-boot system

A dual-boot system is one which offers a choice of operating systems when your computer starts up. If you are already using another operating system, and want to keep it but install Linux as well on the same machine, you have four choices.

1 Make the existing system give up some disk space. If it has more than one hard-disk partition you may be able to sacrifice one and use the space to add Linux.
2 Add a second hard drive.
3 Use a tool such as Partition Magic to shrink an existing partition, releasing some disk space.
4 Reinstall the existing system, but in a smaller partition, leaving enough disk space free for Linux.

Remember to make a backup of all your data before attempting any installation.

The installation process for Linux is reasonably house-trained – it will respect the right of other operating systems it finds on your hard drive to exist. Unfortunately some other systems have installers that simply pillage the entire hard drive for space.

The way around this is to install the other system first. Tell it to divide your hard drive into two partitions, the second one large enough for Linux. When you install Linux use its disk-partitioning tool to delete the second partition and set up Linux in the freed space.

The final stages of the Linux installation will then notice that the other system exists and set up the loader to load either.

Now when you start your computer it will ask you which operating system you want to use, and load whatever you select.

1.7 What to do if installation fails (*optional*)

This section explains some of the causes of installation failure and how to recover from them. You should read it if you have an installation problem and would like to solve it yourself. You should also read it if you are interested in how the hard disk works, how to set up the graphics card or how the computer starts up initially.

Problems with disk partitioning can occur if your hardware is set up incorrectly, if you have unusual hardware or if you are trying to partition the disk to leave room for another operating system.

You can partition the disk manually by entering the cylinder numbers where the individual partitions are to be placed when you get to the partitioning step of the installation.

A hard-disk drive stores information as patterns of magnetism on one or more platters. These are metal disks which are attached to a shaft and spun at high speed. Facing, but not quite touching, each surface of each platter is a head, a device which can read and write the magnetic patterns as the disk rotates, see Figure 1.2. The heads are attached to an access mechanism which moves them across the surfaces of the platters. When the access mechanism stays still each head remains over one ring of information on the spinning disk. This is called a *track*. A track is divided into *sectors*. Because each head is over the corresponding track on a different platter all the information on all of these tracks can be read and written without moving the access mechanism. These tracks taken together are called a *cylinder*. The access mechanism can move the heads into another position where they will be over the tracks of a different cylinder. Cylinders are numbered from 1, which is usually the cylinder closest to the shaft.

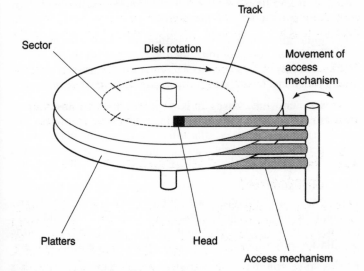

Figure 1.2 Inside a hard drive

The geometry of a hard disk is usually given in the form of three numbers. These are the number of cylinders, the number of heads and the number of sectors per track. Multiplied together these three numbers give the total number of sectors on the disk. The number of sectors multiplied by the number of bytes, roughly the same as characters, which can be stored in each sector gives the capacity of the disk – the amount of information that it can hold. The place where a particular item of information is held is described by three coordinates – the cylinder, head and sector numbers.

When you reach the partitioning step in the installation you can choose to partition the disk manually. The installation program will then give you the choice of a tool such as Disk Druid which has a simple graphical interface or the fdisk program which is more powerful but more difficult to use.

If you have an old machine you should create a boot partition. Ideally this should be at least 10 megabytes in size and created as close to cylinder one as possible. If you want to leave room for upgrades, make this partition about 100 megabytes long. This partition will contain the files used to start the Linux kernel.

Normally you will need to create a swap partition which should be about four times the size of the memory in your computer. For example, if you have 64 megabytes of RAM a suitable size for your swap partition is 256 megabytes.

You should also create a root partition to contain the ordinary files. The *mount points* of the boot and root partitions are /boot and / respectively. You may need to enter these values, which will be explained in a later chapter, if you partition the disk manually.

With unusual video cards it is possible that the installation program may fail to display anything. The way to bypass this problem is to select *text installation* at the beginning of the installation process. You can then add graphics once the basic system is installed.

If the installation process runs to completion but does not set up the graphics card correctly, the result may be a system which goes through the startup sequence and then fails when it should begin to display graphics. The first thing to do in this case is to run the installation procedure but select text rather than graphical login.

At this stage you may have a system which will start up with a text display, but which has no graphics. The next step is to log in as root. At the *login:* prompt enter root and press **Return**. Now enter the root password that you set during installation. If everything works you should now see a *prompt* that ends with the character #. Now type setup and press **Return**. From the menu select 'X Configuration' and follow the instructions. On some more recent distributions this has changed and the command is now

redhat-config-xfree86

on RedHat systems or

sax2

on SuSE.

The new commands have graphical interfaces. The X-Windows system setup (X-Windows) can also be selected from the desktop as

System Settings -> Display

if you are running the RedHat version of GNOME.

Debian systems have a different configuration procedure, explained in Chapter 2.

This will write an *X-Windows configuration file* to your hard disk. You can test this by typing the command startx. This will probably give you working graphics. If not you can use the key combination **Ctrl-Alt-Backspace** (hold down **Ctrl** and **Alt** at bottom left of the keyboard, then press **Backspace** which is normally just above **Return**) to get back to the text screen and try again with different settings.

If in doubt it is usually possible to select 'Generic VGA' for both graphics card and monitor. This will give you a low-resolution display with only 16 colours – poor display quality but enough to allow you to start using the system.

Some installation problems are due to unsupported hardware. It is now rare to find a graphics card that does not work with Linux but some other hardware, notably internal modems, can give problems.

The reason that some hardware is unsupported is either that the manufacturers have failed to release enough information about it, or that it is simply too new for Linux to have caught up with it. In either case the best way to proceed is to get as much of the system as possible working, then search on the internet for software that will work with the troublesome system components.

The hardware databases operated by the distribution manufacturers are an invaluable source of information about hardware that can be made to work with Linux – check the website for the distribution you are using.

The process of starting up a Linux system is explained in Chapter 9, but at this point it is worth mentioning two potential problems. The very first program which is loaded from the hard disk when the system is starting is a boot loader, usually LILO (LInux LOader) or GRUB (GRand Unified Bootloader). This program then attempts to load the kernel into memory and start it. The first potential problem is to do with installing this program. If it is not written correctly to the hard disk during installation the system will not start. The second problem is to do with the way in which the *BIOS* program, which is permanently built into a chip on the motherboard, works. If the boot partition is located beyond cylinder 1023 on the hard disk the BIOS may not be able to read the kernel into memory.

In both cases the solution is to use the recovery disk created during installation. Resetting the computer and allowing it to start up from this disk will get the system up and enable you to solve the problem properly.

Once the system is up the next step is to read the online documentation for the boot loader you are using and follow its suggestions.

1.8 Getting support

There is an extensive and enthusiastic Linux user community which can be contacted both via the internet and through meetings of Local User Groups (LUGs). A list of user groups in the UK can be found at http://www.lug.org.uk/.

User group members, and the regular posters on the Linux discussion groups on the internet, are only too happy to help new users. If the person you first contact cannot solve your particular problem they will almost certainly be able to find someone who can.

There are also mailing lists on the internet, usually associated with specific software packages. These provide a slower, but more targeted form of support. They can usually be found by following links from the websites for the products which they support.

Some LUGs also operate what are called installfests. These are public meetings to which new users are invited to bring their computers. Experts are on hand to sort out installation problems and it is quite common for every new user to leave with a fully working machine.

If you have bought a boxed set with support included you will probably need to register, quoting a number given somewhere inside the box, to receive support. If you have to send in a registration card, rather than registering over the internet, it is a good plan to send the card as soon as you begin trying to install rather than waiting for problems to appear.

EXERCISE

1.7 Search on the internet for your nearest LUG.

1.9 Linux on laptops

Installing Linux on a laptop computer is not very different from installing it on a desktop machine.

There are two pitfalls associated with running Linux on a laptop.

Firstly it is more difficult to find out what chips the makers have used – laptops are not designed to have the graphics card removed for inspection. It is sometimes necessary to bring up a *rescue system* and inspect the /proc file system to find out what hardware is present. This is explained in Chapter 3.

Secondly some thought must be given to the vagaries of battery power. Laptops have a variety of power-saving modes and methods of suspending operations, some of which can interact with Linux in unfortunate ways. It is also worth considering installing a package such as apmd which will write all unsaved information to disk when the battery is close to exhausted.

There is a lot of useful information on installing Linux on laptops at http://www.linux-laptop.net/.

02

the alternatives

In this chapter you will learn:

- how to use the Debian and SuSE distributions
- how to run Knoppix
- how to run Linux on a non-Intel processor

Choosing a Linux distribution is like finding a new house. Everywhere you could choose to live, and each distribution you can buy, has its own collection of advantages. Take your time in choosing, look at several, and you can save yourself the trouble of moving later.

2.1 Debian

Debian is the unconventional distribution. You can learn more about it at http://www.debian.org/. It was created by Ian Murdock in 1993 and named after his wife and himself, Deb–Ian.

The Debian project is run by volunteers, each maintaining a part of the system. Debian does not provide glossy manuals or boxed sets. Debian users load their software from the internet or from recorded – never pressed – CDs.

Debian users often get more out of Linux because they put more in. Freed from marketing constraints the Debian distribution has grown powerful without the emphasis on the graphical interface of the more commercial distributions.

Debian has its own package management system, distinct from Red Hat's package manager (RPM). It is much more potent, if you want to add a new software package it will automatically retrieve from the internet or from CD-ROM any dependencies – other software that you need to load first.

Debian also includes the same networking, sound support and *Graphical User Interface* (GUI) as the other distributions. It offers the choice of both GNOME and KDE desktops.

The volunteers of the Debian project jealously guard the status of their software – everything distributed under the Debian banner is genuinely 'Free Software', it can be freely redistributed, copied and modified. Free in this sense has more to do with freedom of speech than a free lunch.

Debian also exists for a number of different processor families.

2.1.1 Technical differences with Debian (*optional*)

The filesystem layout of Debian is almost the same as the layout of other distributions. The only significant difference you will find is that the System V (SysV) init scripts are in

/etc/init.d not /etc/rc.d/init.d. Curiously some of the other distributions now add *symlinks* (symbolic links) to /etc to hide this difference.

Debian creates the mount points for removable media with names like /floppy rather than /mnt/floppy.

When you install Debian packages – they come in files that end with .deb – you use the apt-get command. For example

```
apt-get install less
```

installs the less package. When I ran this command on the current release of Debian it installed from the file

```
less_374-4_i386.deb
```

which has the version number and platform built into the file name.

Installing a package on Debian configures it, usually by asking the user to set the options for the package.

You can remove a package with

```
apt-get remove packagename
```

and change its configuration by entering:

```
dpkg-reconfigure packagename
```

You must be logged on as root to issue either of these.

2.2 SuSE

SuSE has its own installation tool called *Yet Another Setup Tool* (YAST). YAST displays wonderfully lucid menus – you can learn to use it in about two minutes just by looking at it.

SuSE's installation program is easy to use for simple installations, but it can be a little awkward when setting up a complex multi-boot system. It will decide what it is going to do, and tell you, rather than asking you what you want. If you are doing anything at all unusual it is worth checking everything that the installation program has chosen, and overriding any decisions you do not agree with.

SuSE is rapidly becoming a standard for office and government use throughout Europe. Its clear, no-nonsense desktop and quick, clean installation give it an obvious advantage in this sector.

Users of other systems often find that they can use SuSE with minimal retraining.

2.3 Gentoo

This distribution boots from a single CD, and then creates a build of Linux specially tailored to your hardware.

2.4 Knoppix

This is a build of Debian which will run from a CD *without touching your computer's hard disk.* You can download or buy a Knoppix CD, put it in your CD-ROM drive, restart the machine, and begin experimenting with Linux at once. You can install Linux onto your hard drive from the Knoppix CD later if you choose.

2.5 Non-Intel platforms

Look closely at almost any current processor chip and you will probably find that someone has produced, or at least is developing, a version of Linux to run on it.

The Alpha series of processors manufactured by Compaq (formerly Digital Equipment Corporation) is used in high-performance workstations and servers. Three major distributions – RedHat, Debian and SuSE are available for this processor family. If you want a very powerful computer you should consider running Linux on an Alpha.

The PowerPC family of processors, developed jointly by IBM and Motorola, is used in servers and workstations, and as embedded processors inside other equipment. The main source of information about Linux on the PowerPC is at `http://www.penguinppc.org/`.

Several models of computer, including most of the current Apple Macintosh models and some IBM portables, contain processors in this family. There are also some embedded processor boards from Motorola that use PowerPC chips.

If you have one of these machines you can get Linux distributions from Debian, Gentoo, Mandrake, SuSE and Yellow Dog. Yellow Dog is a PowerPC-specific distribution, see `http://www.yellowdoglinux.com/` for details.

The Motorola 68000 family of processors, usually known as the 68k family, can also run Debian Linux. These processors are found on some embedded cards and in some older Apple computers. You can find some information about this version of Linux at http://www.debian.org/ports/m68k/.

The only problem is that some 68k family processors do not have a Memory Management Unit (MMU). These processors – they usually have EC after the type number – cannot run Linux. If you have some experience with this sort of hardware you may be able to unplug the processor chip from the board and replace it with an MMU version.

03 using linux

In this chapter you will learn:

- what types of data you will find in your files
- how to log into both text and graphical sessions
- how the file tree works
- how to use the Command Language Interpreter
- how to use the different types of files and filesystems
- how to set up and use X-Windows

3.1 Types of data

This section explains the types of data you will find in files on your Linux system. If you have used a computer before you may be familiar with at least some of these.

Computers are made from huge numbers of electronic switches which can be on or off. Internally they use a number system called *binary* which uses only two digits: zero and one. The position of each switch, off or on, represents either a zero or a one. A binary digit is often referred to as a *bit*.

Decimal numbers – the sort we use every day – use the digits zero to nine, and each digit has ten times the significance of the one to its right. This is called working in base ten. Binary numbers work in the same way, except they use base two. Each digit has twice the significance of the one to its right.

The binary number 1011 is 'eight plus two plus one' or in other words eleven in base ten.

Writing numbers in binary makes it clear which switches are on or off, and this is often very useful when working with a computer's hardware. Unfortunately they take a lot of space to write. The number 50,000 in binary is 1100001101010000 – sixteen digits. Because of this it is common practice to write some numbers to base sixteen, this way of writing is called *hexadecimal*. Hexadecimal (often abbreviated to hex) uses the symbols 0–9 and A–F to represent sixteen digits.

Decimal	Binary	Hex	Decimal	Binary	Hex
0	0000	0	10	1010	A
1	0001	1	11	1011	B
2	0010	2	12	1100	C
3	0011	3	13	1101	D
4	0100	4	14	1110	E
5	0101	5	15	1111	F
6	0110	6			
7	0111	7			
8	1000	8			
9	1001	9			

Since the number 16 is $2 \times 2 \times 2 \times 2$ each hexadecimal digit represents exactly four binary digits. By using the table above, a hexadecimal number can be converted to binary and back by eye. The number 50,000 is C350 in hexadecimal. By looking at the table you can convert it to binary:

1100 0011 0101 0000

I have left spaces between the blocks of digits to make this clearer.

Data in files is organized as bytes, binary numbers with eight digits. Because each binary digit can be a zero or a one the number of possible bytes is the same as the result of multiplying eight twos together – 256. A byte is usually used to represent a number in the range 0–255.

Some files contain human-readable text in which one or more bytes represent each character. There are two common ways of arranging this. *Unicode* is slowly gaining acceptance because it can handle the alphabets of many languages at once. However, the older *American Standard Code for Information Interchange* (ASCII) is far more widely used. This can represent the ten digits, the letters of the Roman alphabet and some punctuation marks, storing one character to a byte. It uses byte values 0–31 to represent controls such as tab or newline, 32 is space and 33–126 are printable characters. Value 127 is delete and 128–255 can be used for special characters. The special characters are not standardized and can give unexpected results.

All files contain binary data, even though some data is readable text. It is common practice to use the term 'binary file' to describe any file containing anything that is not text. Examples of binary files are images and sounds.

Files containing programs are of two kinds: the *source* which is the program in a text form which is, with some knowledge, readable by humans. The computer cannot directly understand this form. The source is translated by a program called a *compiler* into an *executable* form. This is a list of simple instructions which the computer can carry out. This form of the program is often referred to as 'the binary'.

3.2 Sessions and logging in

Before using a Linux system you log in by entering a user name and password.

This is both a security feature – unauthorized access to a system can be caught at this point – and a way of identifying the files and settings needed for a particular person's session.

When running on a desktop computer Linux creates a number of text sessions, usually six. This is similar to having six separate text-only computers running at once.

At the same time, if the *X-Windows server* is running, Linux will have a GUI (Graphical User Interface).

You can switch between sessions by pressing **Ctrl-Alt-F1** for the first text session, **Ctrl-Alt-F2** for the second and so on up to **Ctrl-Alt-F6**. **Ctrl-Alt-F7** will then switch back to the GUI.

The text sessions are always present, even though on many systems they will be invisible. The GUI is created by a suite of programs which is optional. It is possible to set up a Linux system which has no graphics; this is sometimes a very useful thing to do.

The GUI can be started in two ways. If you chose graphical login during installation the GUI will appear towards the end of the startup sequence and display a box inviting you to log in. If the system has been set up for text login a text prompt will be come up on the screen, and you can start the GUI with the startx command once you have logged in.

In either case you can enter a user name and password that you set up during installation – this must be done accurately – and you will be logged in.

Once logged in, the system will give you access to your files – which are separate from those of any other user.

The way in which the files are stored is similar to a room full of lockers. The names of the owners of the lockers – the user names – are written on the locker doors. Each owner has a key – the password – which enables them to open only one locker. Within the locker there can be objects – that person's files – and containers such as boxes and bags. The containers are used to keep related objects together and their contents can include more containers, for instance a small box can be kept inside a large one. The owner of the building – the person who can log in as root – has a master key which can be used to open any locker. They can use this master key to help someone who has lost their own key – or forgotten their password. There are also other rooms in the building – equivalent to the files which are owned by the system – which the ordinary people who come in to use the lockers can not see at all.

EXERCISES

3.1 Make sure you can see the GUI login box. Log in using one of the user names you set up during installation. You should now see the desktop for the distribution you are using.

3.2 Run the terminal program. The exact menu selection to do this varies between distributions. It will have an icon that looks like a little monitor and be called either 'Terminal' or 'Shell'. A terminal window will open and you will see a prompt ending in $. Type the letters ps and press the **Return** (sometimes labelled **Enter**) key. You will see a list of the programs you are running.

3.3 Look at the title bar of the window you have opened. Try moving the mouse over the icons in the title bar and then clicking on them to see what they do. Can you find something called 'Help' among the menus? Select it and read the information it provides.

3.4 Press **Ctrl-Alt-F2**. On the text screen log in with the user name root and the root password you set during installation. You will see a prompt ending in the # character. Type who in lower case and press **Return**. This will show that there are two logged-on users: the text session and the GUI.

3.3 The file tree and file paths

All the files known to a Linux system are arranged in a *file tree*. The name comes from the fact that it is arranged as a series of branches fanning out from a single root. Every accessible file and directory, even if it is imported over a network or is on a removable disk, appears somewhere in the tree.

The location of a file in the tree is written as a string of characters called a path.

The file tree begins at the *root directory*. This is usually a directory on your hard disk. The path of the root directory is a single slash character, /. Every other file and directory on the system branches off from the root directory.

A file in the root directory has a path which is a slash followed by the name of the file. So a file called 'information' in the root directory would have /information as its path.

Subdirectories can branch off from the root directory. They have the same type of path as files. For example /etc is a subdirectory that contains a lot of system setup information and /home contains the individual users' files.

The path of a file within a subdirectory is the path of the subdirectory, another slash, and the name of the file. The file that contains a list of the users is /etc/passwd for example.

Further directories can branch off from subdirectories to any number of levels. /home is the directory that contains all the users' files. It can contain /home/kathy which is the files belonging to user kathy – note that the case matters, /home/kathy and /home/Kathy would be two different directories. Then her directory could contain /home/kathy /dogpic.jpg which might well be a picture of her dog in JPEG format. It could also contain /home/kathy/recipes inside which she might keep /home/kathy/recipes /chocolatesauce, /home/kathy/recipes/onionsoup and /home/kathy/recipes/cake.

To save the need to type the full path every time you refer to a file there is a marker which points to one directory in the file tree and says, 'You are here'. Where this marker points is called the *working directory*.

In the example above, if the working directory was set to /home/kathy/recipes the file /home/kathy/recipes /cake could be referred to by nothing more than its name – cake.

The tilde character ~ is a shorthand for 'belongs to'. If Kathy types ~/ this means the same thing as /home/kathy; if Bob types ~/ it means /home/bob. Typing ~kathy/ always means 'where kathy keeps her files', in this case /home/kathy. So ~kathy/recipes/cake means the same as /home/kathy /recipes/cake.

The path ./ refers to the working directory, so in this case ./ means the same as /home/kathy/recipes and can be used as a shorthand for this directory.

A *relative path* is one that is specified as a route from the working directory. The path ../ means 'go back one step towards the root'. So in this case it would mean /home/kathy and ../../ would mean /home. It is possible to extend this, ../../bob would be /home/bob – the directory where Bob keeps his files.

The term *absolute path* is used to distinguish a path that starts at the root, such as /home/kathy/recipes from a relative path.

Files whose names begin with a dot are called hidden files. They are commonly used to hold user preferences and only appear in directory listings if specifically requested with the -a option to ls.

EXERCISES

3.5 If the working directory is /home what is the relative path of
/etc/passwd?

3.6 If the working directory is /home/kathy what is the absolute
path of the file ../bob/kittens.jpg?

3.4 The Command Language
Interpreter (*optional*)

The Command Language Interpreter (CLI) is a mechanism for
controlling the system through commands either typed on a keyboard or read from a file. You may never need to use the CLI.
With current distributions of Linux almost all setup and file
manipulation operations can be done through the GUI.

In the early days of UNIX the CLI was the only way of communicating with a computer. The mouse and the graphical display
had yet to be invented, users sat at Teletype terminals which
printed ten characters per second. Because of this the command
language was made concise to the point of being almost incom-
prehensibly terse. Some of this terseness has been inherited by
Linux.

Almost everything that a Linux system can do has a command
associated with it, so almost everything can be done through the
CLI. Some of the more obscure system functions can only be
reached through the CLI.

CLI commands can be run by other programs. Many of the
graphical tools are simply *graphical front ends* to CLI commands. Click on a button and the graphical tool runs the
command exactly as if it had been typed by a human operator.

The CLI itself can make decisions. It can perform simple tests and
automate repeated operations. There is also a program called
cron that can be set up to run commands at specified times on
particular days.

A CLI command is made up of a word which is used to select a
program or script to run and a list of arguments which tell it what
to do.

For example the command

```
ls /etc
```

tells the CLI to run a program called ls, which lists directories, and to give it the argument /etc to tell it to list the directory with the path /etc.

I suggest you try out these commands as we come to them. Use the terminal window you opened in the previous section. Before you do anything have a look at the prompt. It should end with the dollar sign, $. If it ends with the hash character, #, you are logged in as root, not as an ordinary user – log off and log on again with an ordinary user name.

This check is very important. When logged on as an ordinary user the damage you can do by typing the wrong command is strictly limited and easily repaired. When logged on as root you can do anything – including erasing Linux from your hard disk.

The ls command gives a simple list of the files in a directory but it doesn't tell us anything about the files. Now try typing

```
ls -l /etc
```

then press **Return**. This will give a line of information about each file.

The argument -l is an *option* which the ls program under-stands. With most commands the options either begin with a hyphen and are single letters, or begin with a double hyphen and are words.

This command

```
ls --inode /etc
```

will display the inode number, which is an indicator of how and where the file is stored, for each file.

Now try these commands:

```
ls -l -h /etc
ls -lh /etc
```

Do you see any difference in the output?

The two commands are equivalent. The l option requests long format and the h asks for the file sizes to be converted into a human-readable format. Usually single-letter options can be grouped together after a single hyphen, while word options have to be separated by space and another double hyphen.

There are exceptions to these rules. The command programs have been written by many people over several decades and some commands, notably dd, have their own way of dealing with options. However, the rules are true for nearly all commands.

The program which interprets the typed commands is called a *shell*. There are a number of different shells, with different facilities, available for Linux. One of the most common, and the one you are probably using, is called bash, the Bourne-Again Shell. The name comes from the fact that it is an improved version of an earlier program called the Bourne Shell, named for its author, Stephen Bourne.

The shell understands some of the things you type, and does a little editing before passing them on to the command programs.

To see this happening you can use the echo command. This command simply echoes its arguments. Try it by typing

echo Beware the ides of March

and you will see the message displayed exactly as you typed it.

Now try

echo /etc/*

instead.

What is displayed is the complete list of file and directory names in /etc, the shell has replaced /etc/* with a list of every file name in the /etc directory. This is not exactly readable, or a useful thing to do. But if you combine this with the ls program which does understand files and directories by typing

ls -l /etc/*

you will see every file and the contents of every subdirectory listed.

The output from this command is very long and scrolls off the screen quickly. The next step is to *redirect* the output to another program that can make it readable.

Programs accept input and produce output as *streams*, continuous sequences of characters.

Every program which is run by the shell has streams called *standard input* and *standard output*. These are often abbreviated as stdin and stdout. Standard input is normally the keyboard, standard output is the screen. You can get the shell to send the output somewhere else by using the > character in the command line.

Try this command

```
ls -l /etc/* >dirtxt
```

which will send its output to a file called dirtxt. You may see one or more error messages. These can safely be ignored. They come out through a third stream called *standard error* which can also be redirected.

If you now type

```
ls -l
```

you will see the file dirtxt in your working directory. Note that running ls without specifying a directory makes it list the working directory.

Now type

```
less dirtxt
```

and you will see the contents of the file. Use the up- and down-arrow keys to scroll through the file and the **q** key to quit the program when you have finished.

The two commands can be combined by typing

```
ls -l /etc/* | less
```

where the vertical bar character | is used as a pipe symbol to tell the shell that it should send the standard output of the ls command to the standard input of the less command.

Both commands run at the same time. The ls command will be held up until less is ready to accept its output. Similarly less will be held up until ls produces something for it to display.

Try scrolling up and down with the arrow keys. Try pressing **h** which will show you a help screen. Once again **q** will let you quit from the program.

Use the up-arrow key to recall the last command, then move the cursor into the command with the left arrow and edit the command to read

```
ls -l /etc/* | grep conf | less
```

press **Return** and examine the results. The grep program is a filter which, with the parameter shown, will only let through lines that contain the string 'conf'.

The ability to join programs together in this way is one of the most powerful features of the CLI. The programs really run at the same time. In this example `grep` starts working before `ls` has finished.

The CLI can also run programs one after another. Try this command

```
ls /etc ; ls /
```

the output is the output of the two `ls` commands one after the other.

However, if you type

```
ls /etc & ls /
```

the shell will run both `ls` commands at the same time and the output from both will be jumbled together.

Using a single & symbol at the end of a line is a good way of starting a program, such as an editor, that will open a separate window, and leaving it running.

The next example makes use of the `emacs` editor. Not all distributions install this program by default. If this example does not work at the first attempt you should skip it. In Chapter 8 I will explain how to install additional packages, including this one.

Try this

```
emacs &
```

and you will see the shell display two numbers. The number in square brackets is the *job number* by which the shell keeps track of what is running. The other one is the process ID by which the process you have started – in this case the editor called `emacs` – is known to the system. Note that the prompt is displayed at once, you can type another command while `emacs` is running in the background.

A few seconds later another window will open. This will be the `emacs` editor itself. How to use `emacs` will be explained in Chapter 10 – for the moment you can simply exit from it by clicking on the close box, which is the little cross at top right.

Now go back to the window in which you have been typing commands. Press **Return**. A message will be displayed to tell you that `emacs` has exited.

If you type this command without the &, `emacs` will run in foreground, the shell will not give you a prompt again until `emacs` finishes. You can get around this by pressing **Ctrl-Z**. The shell will pause emacs and let you type another command. If you type

bg

emacs will be moved to the *background* just as if you had typed the &.

Two other useful key combinations are **Ctrl-C** which kills the command running in foreground, and **Ctrl-D** which is an end of file marker. If you run a program which asks you to type several lines of input you can use **Ctrl-D** to tell it that you have finished.

If you have to type a long file name or command you can use tab completion. Type the first few characters and press **Tab**. The shell will then type as many characters as it can, until it reaches a point where it needs you to choose between possibilities. For example type 'showco' and press **Tab**, the shell will complete the command 'showconsolefont'.

The commands man and info are very useful ways of finding out what commands exist and what they do. As an example try typing

man date

which shows the instructions for the date command. The man command displays a single page of information, called a 'man page', through which you can scroll. The info command is more complicated. Many of the pages it displays have menus. Move the cursor onto a menu item, press **Return**, and info will display another page of information.

You can turn a man page into a printable file by adding the -t option. For example

man -t mv | lpr

will print the man page for the mv command.

There are a huge number of commands that can be executed from the CLI, and every software package added to the system supplies more. At the last count there were over 1700 commands available on the machine I am using to write this book.

The following list contains the commands you will need most often, together with a short description of what each one does and an example. In each case the parts of the command which are always the same are shown in lower case, the places in which you substitute your own file names are shown in CAPITALS.

- `cp SOURCE DESTINATION`
  copies a file from the path `SOURCE` to the path `DESTINATION`. The original file is unchanged, the destination file is an exact copy of it.

  Example: `cp old.text new.text`

  This makes a copy of the file `old.text` and puts the copy in a new file called `new.text`.

- `ln -s SOURCE DESTINATION`
  Instead of copying the file this command makes a *symbolic link* from the destination to the source. When you look at the destination directory with the

  `ls -l`

  command you will see a pointer symbol and the name of the file that the link points to. You can use the symbolic link (often abbreviated to symlink) as if it were the file it references.

- `mv SOURCE DESTINATION`
  moves the file with the path `SOURCE` to the path `DESTINATION`. The original file vanishes. This can be used to move a file to a different directory or to rename a file within a directory.

  Example: `mv this.data that.data`

  renames the file `this.data` in the current directory to `that.data`.

  Example: `mv ./raw/fish.pic ./cooked/lunch.pic`

  moves the file `fish.pic` from the subdirectory `raw` to the subdirectory `cooked`, renaming it to `lunch.pic` at the same time.

- `rm PATH`
  Remove, in other words permanently delete, the file `PATH`. More than one path can be given, separated with spaces, in which case all the paths will be removed. Note that in most cases the data in the files *cannot* be recovered after this operation. The `-r` option will make `rm` remove directories, their contents and their subdirectories – it should be used with extreme caution.

  Example: `rm file_of_old_stuff file_not_wanted`

  This command will remove `file_of_old_stuff` and `file_not_wanted` from the current directory.

- mkdir DIRECTORY
  This creates a new directory with the path DIRECTORY. The new directory is empty.

  Example: mkdir toybox

  This creates a new directory called toybox in the current directory.

- rmdir DIRECTORY
  This removes a directory – deletes it permanently. The directory must be empty. To check for a directory being empty use the command

  ls -a DIRECTORY

  and if it is empty you will only see the entries for the directory you are looking at (a single dot) and its parent directory (two dots).

  Example: rmdir toybox

  This removes the directory called toybox.

- cat FILES
  This command takes any number of paths separated by spaces, reads all the files and sends their contents to standard output. The files it reads are unchanged.

  Example: cat fred jim wombat

  This sends the contents of the files fred, jim and wombat to the screen.

  Example: cat fred jim >joinedup

  This creates a new file called joinedup and puts the contents of fred and jim into it.

- pwd
  This command 'prints' the path of the current working directory to the screen. The word 'print' in this case is an historical relic of the printing terminals on older UNIX systems – it does not in fact send anything to the printer.

- cd PATH
  This command changes the current working directory to PATH.

  Example: cd toybox

  This changes the current working directory to toybox.

Example: cd ..

This changes the working directory to its parent. If the working directory is /home/bob/toybox/thing this command will change it to /home/bob/toybox.

EXERCISES

3.7 Create a subdirectory called testfiles.

3.8 Use the date command to see the current date and time.

3.9 Run the date command again, but redirect its output to ./testfiles/date1 – use the > redirection operator.

3.10 Change the working directory to testfiles.

3.11 Once again run the date command, sending its output to a file called date2 in the working directory.

3.12 Examine the contents of date1 and date2 with less. What happens if you do this:

```
less date1 date2
```

which gives both file names to less?

3.13 Create a file which contains the information in date1 and date2 joined together. Do this by redirecting the output of the cat command.

3.5 Filesystems

Linux can access filesystems in a variety of formats. It has its native formats but it can understand FAT, Macintosh HFS, ISO 9660 (CD-ROM), OS/2 HPFS and many others.

A filesystem exists on a device which can be a removable disk such as a floppy or a disk cartridge. A device can also be a partition on a hard drive or the whole of the drive. It can be an area of RAM or even a file within another filing system. On networked machines a filesystem on another computer, accessed over the network, can be mounted as if it were a device.

For the files on a device to be accessed by Linux the device must be *mounted* with the mount command. When the kernel mounts a device it reads some information about how to access files on that device and keeps it in memory. After accessing the files on a device it must be *unmounted*. This makes the computer put any changed information it is holding back on the device.

There are some enormous advantages to having a formal mount and unmount mechanism. The major one is that it makes 'lazy write' safe. When an application program wants to write a file to disk the file is quite often small enough to sit in the computer's main memory for a while. It can then be written to the disk later, when the computer is less busy.

If the disk is taken out of the drive before the file has been written the file will never find its way onto the disk. The umount command, which unmounts a disk, forces Linux to write all unwritten data to the disk. With removable disks (other than floppies) it does not unlock the eject mechanism until this operation is complete. Umount will not work if any tasks are using the disk you are trying to unmount. You can use the command

```
fuser -m /filesystem
```

or

```
lsof /filesystem
```

as root to find out which tasks are hanging onto the filesystem you want to unmount. Lsof produces more intelligible output.

All the files which are known to a Linux system appear in a file tree. When a device is mounted the directories and files on that device are grafted onto the file tree at a point which is called the *mount point*. A mount point is a directory which already exists in the file tree. For example if you have a floppy which contains files called wom.bat and fruit.bat, and a directory called bats, and you mount this floppy at the mount point /mnt/floppy, the files will appear as /mnt/floppy/wom.bat and /mnt/floppy/fruit.bat, the directory on the floppy will be /mnt/floppy/bats.

The directory which is used as a mount point should be empty. Once a filesystem is mounted on it, any files already in the directory used as mount point effectively vanish until the filesystem mounted on it is unmounted again.

Most GUIs include tools for mounting and unmounting filesystems. You can use these and ignore the CLI commands.

In a terminal window, type

```
cat /etc/fstab
```

to see the file which contains a list of filesystems. This table is used to simplify mounting and unmounting commonly used systems.

It contains entries for filesystems which are mounted when the system starts up and for filesystems which can be mounted and unmounted by the running system.

The information is arranged in six columns, see Figure 3.1. The first column is the location of the filesystem to mount. This can be written in a variety of ways.

- A *special file* describing a disk or disk partition to mount. The first IDE disk is /dev/hda, the second is /dev/hdb and so on. SCSI disks are /dev/sda, /dev/sdb, as are USB devices – Linux treats USB as being a special type of SCSI. Where a disk is partitioned a number is added to the end of the special file name to select the partition number. So, in Figure 3.1, /dev/hda8 is partition eight on the first IDE hard disk. Note that the floppy on this computer (a laptop) is an external USB device and so it appears as /dev/sda. If it had been a conventional floppy it would have been /dev/fd0.
- A label. This label is written to a disk partition when the filesystem is first created on it. Linux will search all available partitions for a matching label.
- The word 'none'. This is used for some filesystems which do not live on real devices but are used to access parts of the kernel.
- A description of where to find a filesystem over the network. The string falstaff:/home describes the filesystem /home on the machine whose name on the network is falstaff.

The next column lists the mount points where the filesystems are mounted. The root filesystem is mounted on /, a mount point which always exists. All the other mount points must be either directories within that filesystem, or directories on other mounted filesystems.

The third column indicates the type of filesystem. Linux has its own filesystems, known as ext2 and ext3 – the second and third extended filesystems. The original extended filesystem is obsolete. The difference between ext2 and ext3 is that ext3 has a journal, an area of the disk in which the system makes notes about what is changing on the disk. Because of this a computer which uses ext3 can recover its disks in seconds after a power failure, rather than the minutes which recovering ext2 takes. The filesystems which access the kernel, such as proc, have their own types. Filesystems which are accessed over a network have

```
[unclebob@titania unclebob]$ cat /etc/fstab
LABEL=/             /               ext3    defaults                        1 1
LABEL=/boot         /boot           ext3    defaults                        1 2
none                /dev/pts        devpts  gid=5,mode=620                   0 0
/dev/hda8           /exchange       vfat    defaults,umask=0                 0 0
none                /proc           proc    defaults                        0 0
none                /dev/shm        tmpfs   defaults                        0 0
/dev/hda6           swap            swap    defaults                        0 0
/dev/cdrom          /mnt/cdrom      iso9660 noauto,owner,kudzu,ro           0 0

falstaff:/home      /falstaff       nfs     noauto,user                     0 0
falstaff:/workspace /workspace      nfs     noauto,user                     0 0
/dev/sda            /mnt/floppy     auto    noauto,owner,kudzu              0 0
[unclebob@titania unclebob]$
```

Figure 3.1 The file /etc/fstab

nfs as their type. This stands for 'Network File System' and will be explained in Chapter 6. Vfat is a generic term for the fat filesystem and its variants which are used by MS-DOS and systems derived from it. The swap filesystem is an area of disk in which the kernel can place tasks which are temporarily idle in order to reclaim the memory they are using. CD-ROMs use the ISO 9660 filesystem – the name comes from the International Standards Organization publication which defines the layout of data on a CD-ROM.

Finally the filesystem type can be set to 'auto'. In this case the system will, by trial and error, try to find out what filesystem is present on a device. Put a floppy in MS-DOS, ext2, ext3 or Macintosh HFS format in the drive, click on the appropriate icon and the system will mount it correctly.

In the fourth column is a list of the options for each filesystem. In most cases this is simply the word 'defaults', indicating that the default options – to mount the filesystem when the computer starts up – are all that is needed. You can find a list of the options you can use here on the man page for the 'mount' command. Filesystems marked 'user' can be mounted and unmounted by any logged-on user, the 'owner' option means that only the person logged using the screen and keyboard connected to the computer can mount and unmount them, not a user who is logged on over the network from another machine.

Some filesystems, such as ext2 and ext3, make a note of which user owns each file, and keep a list of permissions – things that different users are allowed to do to the file. Application programs expect this information to be present, regardless of the type of the filesystem. Some filesystems hold neither owner information nor a complete set of permissions. Because of this, extra information often has to be supplied in the options when mounting a filesystem such as fat or vfat.

The fifth column of fstab controls backups – it is rarely used.

The sixth and last column is used to select the checks that Linux makes at startup. A 1 in this column means that the filesystem is checked for damage before the bulk of the system is started. The root filesystem should be marked with a 1. A 2 means that the filesystem is checked as part of the routine startup sequence and is the normal setting for all other partitions on fixed disks. A 0 in column six means that Linux will not do any automatic checks.

Some filesystems can be mounted *read-only*. Programs can read files on these filesystems but all attempts to write are vetoed by the kernel. CD-ROMs which cannot be written are always mounted read-only. You can mount any device read-only. This is sometimes a very useful thing to do if you want to let many users have access to data that must not be changed.

Mounting a filesystem with the noexec option prevents Linux from running any programs it finds on that filesystem. You can use this option if you want to mount a CD-ROM that you do not entirely trust, for example. You will be able to read all the files on the CD, but your computer will refuse to run any programs it finds there unless you explicitly copy them somewhere else first.

The Hierarchical File System (HFS) used on some Apple Macintosh machines can be used on Linux. Files on an HFS disk have two parts, the data fork and the resource fork. If you mount an HFS volume on a Linux machine the data fork of each file will appear as a normal file. In each directory there will be a hidden subdirectory called .resource, which will contain the same filenames as its parent directory. The files in .resource will contain the resource forks of those files.

There is an array of programs with names that begin mkfs that you can use to create filesystems, either on removable disks or partitions on hard drives. There is one program for each filesystem type. For example mkfs.ext3 creates an ext3 filesystem, mkfs.vfat creates a vfat filesystem, and so on.

Remember that any of these programs will erase all the data on the disk or partition it is working on.

3.6 The /proc filesystem

The kernel keeps track of running processes, hardware and loaded modules. You can access this information through a special filesystem called /proc. The files in this system do not exist, the file names are really gateways to system data.

The numbered entries refer to processes. You can find out about everything that is running on your computer by looking here.

The /proc/pci file is a list of the hardware that is plugged in to your computer's PCI bus. This will usually tell you what chips you have on your motherboard and interface boards. You can use it to work out which drivers you need for your hardware. The same information is in /proc/bus/pci/devices, but as raw numbers rather than readable text. Similarly under /proc/scsi/ you will find information about SCSI devices and under /proc/bus/usb about USB devices.

3.7 Special files

Directory entries can refer to things other than files. They can be *First In, First Out* (FIFO) character queues, used to transfer data from one application to another.

You can connect to the device drivers, small programs which transfer data to and from hardware devices, by reading and writing *special files*. These files, which usually live in the /dev directory, are created with the mknod command. They contain two numbers. The *major number* associates a special file with a driver, and the *minor number* with a particular device handled by that driver.

For example /dev/tty0 and /dev/tty1 share the major number 4 – they are both handled by the serial driver. They have different *minor numbers*, in this case 0 and 1 because they refer to different hardware – the two serial ports on your computer.

The device /dev/null is created by the system. Anything you write to it is permanently lost, any attempt to read from it returns a zero-length file. There are several internal devices like this, /dev/zero returns zeroes and /dev/random supplies random numbers, for example.

3.8 X-Windows

3.8.1 Client–server windowing

The X-Windows system is the foundation of all GUIs used with Linux. The components of X-Windows are the *server*, one or more *clients*, a *window manager*, and optionally a *display manager*.

The server is the program that operates the display hardware. It looks after your mouse and keyboard, and tells your graphics card what to display.

The display manager is optional. It is the program that puts up the login screen and arranges it so that when a user logs in, ownership – and therefore complete control – of the display is given to that user. If the system is set up to use text login, rather than a login screen, the display manager may not be present at all.

Clients are application programs, for example terminal emulators, games and word processors.

Clients display their windows by connecting to a server and sending it messages. These messages tell the server to draw simple objects such as lines, rectangles and text. More complicated objects, such as buttons and text-entry boxes, are called *widgets* and are created by library software that joins together the simple objects to make complex ones. The common widget libraries include Qt, Motif, OpenLook and Athena.

Because the connection between client and server is a normal socket connection – the same as any connection made over a network – the client and server do not have to be on the same computer.

You can run a program on one computer and have its displays appear on another. This lets you borrow processor speed by running a program on a lightly loaded machine elsewhere in the network.

The client only provides the 'inside' part of its windows. The borders, title bar and system menu are added by the window manager. Because of this an application may change its look and feel when moved from one machine to another.

3.8.2 Advanced X-Windows (*optional*)

This section covers the mechanics of connecting to a server and the way window managers and clients interact. You should read it if you intend to do anything other than the simplest operations with X-Windows, or if you intend to use X-Windows over a network.

An application program that uses X-Windows uses a library, known as *xlib*, to access one or more servers. Xlib manages messages sent to and received from the servers.

When a program that uses xlib starts up, xlib looks in a few standard places to find out which display it should use. It will look at the DISPLAY environment variable and usually at the -display command line option. Either of these can describe a display in this way:

```
falstaff:0.0
```

where falstaff, for example, is the name on the network of the computer the display is connected to. A blank name, :0.0, means the display on the computer you are using. Some computers have more than one display, keyboard and mouse. The first number after the colon is the number of the display, counting from zero. One display can be split over two or more monitors by using multiple graphics cards. The number after the dot is the number of the monitor to use, once again counting from zero. In many cases the dot and the second number are not needed.

The DISPLAY variable is set automatically when using X-Windows on a single machine. If you want to log into a remote machine and run programs that use your display you must make sure that it is set to refer to the display you are looking at. Connecting to a remote machine with telnet or ssh can set the variable correctly. If not, you can set the DISPLAY variable with this command:

```
export DISPLAY=host:0.0
```

A server will not automatically accept a connection from any other machine. This is an important security feature: it prevents other users on the same network seeing what is on your screen.

The simplest way of controlling access to your display, and one that is reasonably satisfactory on a very small, secure network is to use the xhost program. This program sends commands to the server to tell it to accept or reject connections from particular computers. It does not offer good enough security to control access to displays over the public internet. If you use ssh instead of telnet you will usually find that authentication is done for you, and you do not need to use xhost.

When a client (an application program) connects to a server the client supplies, via the connection, the 'inside' parts of a window. The borders and title bar are added by the window manager. The window manager can also move, iconize and resize windows.

To see this in action you can start and stop window managers while applications continue to run. The window managers built into KDE and GNOME are not entirely suitable for this, but you can use two older and simpler managers, twm and mwm, to demonstrate the mechanism.

Before this demonstration you must shut down the display manager and the server. Log in as root and use the telinit command to change the system runlevel so that the system switches over to text-based login.

On Red Hat systems this is runlevel 3, and the command to type is:

```
telinit 3
```

On Debian systems stopping the display manager service has the same effect.

You may have to log in again. Once again log in as root.

Next try the effect of starting the X-Windows server with no clients. Type this command:

```
X
```

Note that it is a capital X and takes no parameters.

The X server will start and you will see the display switch into graphical mode. No windows will open and there will be no background. The only thing on the screen will be the mouse cursor.

Press **Ctrl-Alt-Backspace** (**Backspace** is at top right of the main part of the keyboard) to quit from the server and return to a text screen.

This is what the server on its own, with no clients, looks like.

Now type

```
xinit
```

once again with no parameters. The display will switch back into graphical mode. The xinit command is a script which both starts the X server and runs the terminal emulator, then waits for the terminal emulator to exit and shuts down the server.

You will now see a terminal window, but it will have no borders or title bar. This is what happens if you have both a server and a client running but no window manager.

Move the mouse cursor over the terminal window and type

```
twm &
```

to start the tab window manager. This is one of the older window managers and only has a few, very basic, features. Putting the & symbol at the end of the command makes it run in background so that you can type more commands.

Now type

```
xterm &
```

to start a second terminal emulation. You will need to click the left mouse button once to make twm place the window on the screen.

The next step is to quit twm. Click the left mouse button with the cursor over the background and select 'Exit' from the menu. The decorations around the windows will vanish.

In one of the terminal windows type

```
mwm &
```

and new decorations, this time in the style of the Motif window manager will appear. Click the right mouse button on the background this time to display the menu and quit from the window manager.

The desktop environments are nothing more than complex window managers combined with applications that display icons and menus.

If you have the *GNOME* desktop environment installed you can try typing

```
gnome-session
```

to start the GNOME desktop. Be aware that the desktop environments are complex programs and may not behave quite correctly when started from a text session.

To exit from the desktop simply select 'Log Out' from the system menu.

The xinit script waits for the first application it starts to exit. Type

```
exit
```

in each of the terminal windows and you will see the server shut down and return the screen to a text session.

Now either use the telinit program to return to graphical login (on RedHat and SuSE systems this is runlevel 5) or reboot your computer with this command:

```
shutdown -r now
```

Log in again, as an ordinary user.

The server sends messages to clients to tell them about events, such as mouse movements and keystrokes. You can see these messages by opening a terminal window and typing this command:

```
xev
```

A second window will open. In the terminal window you will see all the event messages sent to the second, event-tester, window. Try moving the mouse, clicking inside and outside the window, and pressing keys to see how the messages are structured.

3.8.3 Configuring X-Windows (*optional*)

When an X-Windows server starts up it reads a configuration file called /etc/X11/XF86Config. This file is created by the installation process. There are also some tools, which vary between distributions, that can change this file in a running system.

In common with most configuration files in Linux systems this file is plain text, and can be edited with any text editor. If you want to experiment with editing this file you should first make a copy of a version of the file that is known to work – copy it to XF86Config.working or some similar name – so that you can safely reinstate the system if your changes stop the display working.

The exact format of this file is documented. You can see the documentation with the command

man XF86Config

Note the capital letters in the name.

The file contains a number of parameters, many of which can be ignored. If you have a very unusual graphics card or monitor you can adjust the graphics to work properly by making manual changes to this file. Some graphics cards have the unfortunate habit of failing completely if they are given an incorrect parameter. If you suspect that this may have happened, simply copy the last known working backup of XF86Config back to its original name and location, then try again. If the graphics card still does not work, shut down the computer and switch off, wait a few seconds and switch on again.

All the colours which can be displayed on a screen are made up from mixtures of red, green and blue light. Red and blue together give a purplish colour called magenta; green and red give yellow; all three at once make white. The screen is divided into tiny dots called picture elements or pixels. A graphics card tells the monitor how much red, green and blue light to show at each pixel. Some graphics cards can adjust the brightness of each colour at every point on the screen. Others can only display a limited range of colours chosen from a palette.

A running server offers one or more visuals to its clients. A visual describes what the graphics card can do – how many colours it can display and what sort of palette, if any, it uses. Clients are then expected to send requests to the server in a way that fits in with the visual. The server may allow the clients to send requests in several different forms, in which case the server will offer the client a choice of several visuals.

You may sometimes see error messages with the word 'visual' in them, particularly if a program cannot start up because it cannot find a visual it can use.

If this happens, use the xdpyinfo command to look at the visuals the server offers. You can then change the XF86Config file, as described above, to reconfigure the server so that it offers a visual that the program can use. Remember that changes only take effect when the server is stopped and restarted – you can force this by pressing **Ctrl-Alt-Backspace**, but make sure you close any programs with unsaved data first. It is only the server that needs to be restarted, there is no need to reboot the machine.

EXERCISES

3.14 Use the less command to examine the file /etc/X11 /XF86Config. Read the manual page for this file.

3.15 Use the xdpyinfo command to read information about your display. Compare what you find with the result of the previous exercise.

3.9 The Graphical User Interface (GUI)

In the previous sections you have seen how the X-Windows system works. X-Windows is only the foundation of the GUI, it operates the graphics card and deals with the keyboard and mouse. As a user you want more than this. You want to be able to drag and drop files, run applications by clicking on them and keep track of open windows.

There are several desktop environments that can be run on X-Windows. The older fvwm is rarely used now. The two commonest are KDE and GNOME. You can learn more about KDE and GNOME at http://www.kde.org/ and http://www.gnome.org/ respectively, which are the official project websites.

Both KDE and GNOME offer similar features. You can use them to drag and drop files between different directories, mount and unmount filesystems with your mouse and start programs from menus.

There are some technical differences between KDE and GNOME, and the features they offer are slightly different. I suggest that you install both, try them out and decide which you like.

Linux makes a distinction between different users, and between users and root. Because of this each user has their own preferences, stored in hidden files and directories in their home directory.

EXERCISES

3.16 Visit the websites `http://www.kde.org/` and `http://www.gnome.org/` and compare the features of KDE and GNOME.

3.17 Using either KDE or GNOME – preferably both – use a text editor to create a file containing a short message. Mount a floppy, copy the text file onto it. Unmount the floppy.

3.18 Both KDE and GNOME display some files on the desktop. Find out what the path of one of these files is – you may find that both the online help and the `find` command are useful.

3.19 Use the CLI to create a file on the desktop. Does the GUI display it at once? If the GUI that you are using has an option to refresh the desktop, what does it do?

04

software that runs on linux

In this chapter you will learn:

- how to use office applications
- how to set up, connect and use databases
- about the different types of graphical tools
- about the different types of available applications
- how to play games on Linux
- how to access the internet from Linux

Linux has inherited a lot of applications, such as the Tex type-setting system and the vi and emacs editors from classical UNIX. Much of this older software is useful, but not quite what is wanted in the modern office or home environment.

Over the past few years several software vendors have produced high-quality applications for Linux. This is a representative, but by no means complete, selection.

4.1 Office applications

Office applications include tools for creating and manipulating text documents and graphics, and for organizing information.

There is no shortage of office applications for Linux. As a new user you are more likely to have trouble choosing between a plethora of alternatives than to fail to find a package to do what you want.

Linux lends itself to almost seamless office integration. Figure 4.1 shows how you can join together standard components to make an integrated office. All the software needed to do this is included in most major distributions, and can be downloaded from the internet.

You can set up one or more databases to keep track of friends, pets, holidays, finances and sports. You can use *Structured Query Language* (SQL) to access your data. This is a nominally standard way of connecting to a database. It uses queries for-matted in a mixture of English words and mathematical symbols to store, retrieve, search and sort data. I will explain SQL in a later section.

SQL databases can very easily be shared across a network. You can set up an SQL server on one computer and have users on several machines access it, a useful thing to do if you want to dis-tribute data across an office, for example.

The alternative is to use dBase databases – the name derives from an earlier program that used this database format. These are much simpler, do not share between machines and cannot handle complex queries. They are much easier to set up – a dBase data-base is simply a few files on your computer – and are more than adequate for home use.

OpenOffice is likely to become the standard office suite by default, as it is beginning to be included with distributions.

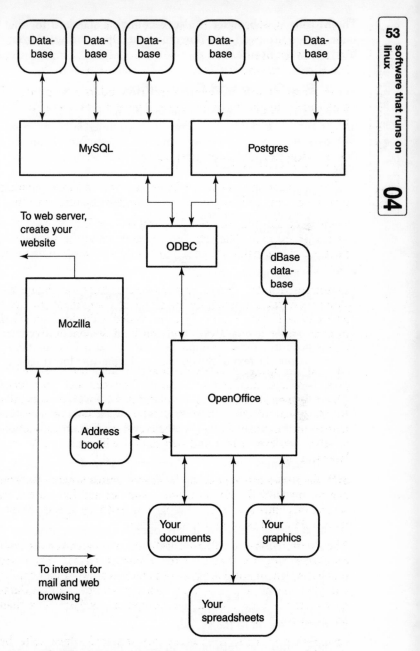

Figure 4.1 Office, internet and database integration

The Mozilla web browser is also becoming a standard for the same reason. You can also download the Opera browser from `http://www.opera.com/`.

4.1.1 StarOffice and OpenOffice

These started as the same package and still have a lot of features in common. StarOffice is now sold commercially by Sun Microsystems, `http://www.sun.com`. OpenOffice can be downloaded free of charge from `http://www.openoffice.org`.

Both packages include:

- Writer – a word processor.
- Calc – a spreadsheet.
- Draw – a vector graphics tool.
- Impress – a slideshow package.
- Math – an equation editor.

These packages can both import and export word-processor documents and spreadsheets in Microsoft-proprietary formats.

Their native file format uses compression – a document saved in OpenOffice format can be unpacked with the `unzip` command to separate out the text of the document, formatting information and embedded graphics.

OpenOffice can merge data from a variety of sources, such as the Mozilla address book, spreadsheets and dBase databases, into word-processor documents. It can also connect to several types of shared database.

OpenOffice comes with a full help system. Most of its windows, including popups, have a 'Help' selection that takes you to the relevant documentation.

Most of OpenOffice is so easy to use, and so well documented, that the easiest way to learn it is to open a word-processor document, a drawing or a spreadsheet and experiment with the menu options.

The slideshow program, called Impress, shares many features with Draw, the graphics program. The easiest way to learn both is to tackle the graphics program first, and when you are familiar with it move on to the slideshow.

The three buttons at bottom left in the graphics program which let you add layers to drawings, and create a 'Master Drawing' that appears on all pages, take on a special significance when used with a slideshow. You can use layers to build up a drawing, a little at a time, as the slideshow proceeds. The 'Master' selection lets you add such things as the presentation title and your company logo to every slide.

OpenOffice makes use of 'Registered Data Sources', an easy way of making different types of database available to any application you are using.

A database is a collection of one or more tables. A table is a list of records. Each record in a table has one or more fields – places that hold the data. The layout of the fields is the same for each record in a table.

When you display a database, each record is shown as one line of cells, each cell containing one field for that record. Each field of each record is shown lining up with the corresponding field in the record above and the one below.

This is why a record is sometimes called a *row* and the data in the same field in every record a *column*.

This is a very simple example of a table, an incomplete star catalogue containing a half-dozen of the brightest. There are rows displaying records for the six named stars. Each record has three fields – the name of the star, its magnitude (note that a smaller magnitude means a *brighter* star) and its spectral type. The fields are displayed as three columns.

Name	Magnitude	Type
Betelgeuse	0.8	M2
Rigel	0.11	B8
Vega	0.04	A0
Deneb	1.25	A2
Sirius	−1.45	A1
Arcturus	−0.06	K2

In either Writer or Calc you can select

Tools → Data Sources...

to bring up a dialogue window that lets you connect to various data sources.

These are the kinds of data source you can use:

- Adabas. This is a commercial database produced by Software AG in Darmstadt, Germany. See http://www.softwareag.com/ for details. Use this selection if you already have an Adabas database.
- JDBC. This is Java Database Connectivity. Use this selection if JDBC is already installed on your system or network.
- ODBC. Open Database Connectivity is an extra layer of software that sits between an application, such as OpenOffice, and one or more databases. It is supposed to iron out the differences between SQL implementations, but it needs some setting up. This is described in a later section. Install ODBC if you want to use pre-existing SQL databases or if you want to add shared databases to your system.
- dBase. This is the simplest form of database. You can create a dBase database using the Data Sources tool in Writer or Calc.
  1 Click on the 'New Data Source' button.
  2 Enter a name for your database.
  3 Set 'Database Type' to dBase.
  4 In the URL box enter a full path, such as /home/ yourname/yourdatabase. This will be created as a directory, and every table in the database will be a file in this directory.
  5 Click on the 'Tables' tab. If you have set everything up correctly the directory will be created, and an empty table list will appear.
  6 Click on 'New Table Design' – the icon with the little yellow asterisk.
  7 Design your database. Give each field a name in the first column, choose the type of data that goes in it in the second column and use the third for optional notes explaining what the field is for.
  8 Save the database by clicking on the floppy disk icon. You will be asked to give your table a name, type in something suitable.
  9 Close the database design window.
- Text. Some database packages can export a table as plain text, with individual values separated by commas or tab characters. OpenOffice can import this sort of table if you use this selection.
- Spreadsheet. You can use a spreadsheet as data source. The first row of the spreadsheet becomes the field names, and the rest of the sheet contains the data.

- AddressBook. OpenOffice can connect to an address database in several standard formats. You can use this to integrate the address book built into the Mozilla browser with OpenOffice. Use the address book tools in Mozilla to create as many address books as you would like for business contacts, club members, suppliers, customers, friends and enemies. You can now use the same address book with the Mozilla e-mail client and OpenOffice to send both e-mails and printed letters to the people in your address books.

OpenOffice has a tool for creating forms. You can add a form to any word-processor document or spreadsheet.

A form is an object that spreads a database record out into a whole page of data so that it is more readable. It also simplifies data entry.

The quickest way to make a form is to start by adding a 'Table Control' box to a word-processor document. Click and hold the mouse on the 'Form' button (near the top on the left side of the window) and drag to the right until the popup help box says 'Table Control'. The program will now ask you which table is used to control your form. Select the appropriate database and table. Choose which fields are to appear in the box.

The 'Table Control' box will let you select a record from the database by scrolling through a list.

Now add other boxes to the form. You can attach these to fields in the database. Click the right mouse button on the background and select 'Control...' from the menu to open the properties dialogue. Then select a box by clicking on it and click the 'Data' tab in the dialogue. You can now use the 'Data field' drop-down menu to connect a data field to your new box.

When you are happy with your new form you can save it just like any other document.

On the second row of controls which come up when you click and drag on the 'Form' button, select 'Design Mode On/Off'.

Your form will now come to life. All the boxes and buttons will start working and you can use them to enter real data.

OpenOffice has an *Application Programming Interface* (API) which you can use to create new dialogues and commands. I use the word 'can' with some caution. The API manual is over 900 pages long and explains how to write C, Java and BASIC programs that add new features to OpenOffice. You can download the manual from `http://api.openoffice.org/` in PDF format.

EXERCISE

4.1 Using either OpenOffice or StarOffice create the table of stars as a dBase database. Why does the magnitude column have to be text, not numeric? Create a form that lets you add new stars to the table.

4.1.2 Applix office suite

I can personally recommend this package as I am using it to write this book. In the five years or so that I have been an Applix user I have produced documents totalling well over three hundred thousand words and it has never once let me down. At the time of writing it is still available, but not being actively maintained.

4.1.3 SQL databases (*optional*)

Structured Query Language (SQL) is a way of accessing databases which is supposed to be standard. However, there are some differences between servers – the programs that manage the databases. To get around this, and to provide a standard programming interface, the ODBC package includes drivers for most common database servers. When you run a program that uses ODBC it will behave in the same way regardless of which database it is connected to.

Setting up an SQL database is straightforward. The only problem you may encounter is that a great many setup errors, such as missing drivers, result in a program crashing with either no explanation or an error message which is cryptically obscure. The real solution to this is to get the setup instructions for the package you are using and follow every step to the letter.

The basic SQL syntax varies slightly between databases. One of the most confusing differences is that the mysql monitor has a SHOW DATABASES and a SHOW TABLES command whereas the psql monitor used by PostgreSQL does not. Instead PostgreSQL creates database tables called pg_databases and pg_tables which contain the same information and can be examined with the SELECT command.

The package SQL-Ledger at `http://www.sql-ledger.org/` is a complete small-business accounting suite which uses an SQL database.

4.1.3.1 Setting up a PostgreSQL database

You can set up a PostgreSQL database by installing both the basic database software and the server itself. These are commonly two separate packages.

When you start the PostgreSQL server it will listen on a UNIX-domain socket for client programs to come along and access its databases. If you want to access the server across a network from another machine, or from a package that does not use UNIX-domain sockets, you can add the TCP/IP address domain by editing /var/lib/pgsql/data/postgresql.conf. Uncomment these lines – note that they may vary slightly between versions of the server:

```
tcpip_socket = true
port = 5432
hostname_lookup = false
show_source_port = false
```

Start the server by using the the 'Server Settings' option on the desktop or typing

```
service postgresql start
```

in the shell – you must be logged in as root to do this.

The PostgreSQL server does not run as root. When it is installed it creates a *pseudo user* called postgres. To control the server you can either log in as postgres, or su to postgres from another login. Then you can use these commands to control the server:

- createuser – Make a new entry in the list of users allowed to access the database.
- dropuser – Remove a user from the list.
- createdb – Create a database.
- dropdb – Remove a database.

Once you have one user and one database set up you can use the psql program to test the database by typing SQL commands. The details of SQL itself are beyond the scope of this book, but the command

```
select * from pg_databases ;
```

will display the contents of the list of databases and demonstrate that the system is working.

Access to the postgres server is controlled by the file /var/lib/pgsql/data/pg_hba.conf. This specifies which machines can connect to the server, and how the identity of the person logging on is checked. This file contains a lot of helpful comments.

The full documentation for PostgreSQL is available in a variety of formats from `http://www.postgresql.com/`, including an excellent SQL tutorial.

4.1.3.2 Setting up a MySQL database

Install the `mysql`, `mysql-server` and `mysql-devel` packages, or their equivalents, and start the `mysql` server.

MySQL comes with extensive documentation in the form of a single gargantuan HTML file. This contains a very useful SQL tutorial. You can leave this open in a browser on one desktop while you experiment with SQL in a window on another.

Use the command `mysql`, with no parameters, to open the `mysql` monitor. MySQL starts up with two databases already created:

- `mysql` – This is the database of users and their access rights. Use the GRANT and REVOKE commands to modify it.
- `test` – This is a scratch area where you are free to try out SQL commands without damaging any real data.

4.1.3.3 Setting up ODBC

Install the `unixODBC` and `unixODBC-devel` packages. Add the drivers (MyODBC or PostgreSQL-odbc).

The relationships between the names that ODBC gives to databases, the drivers, and the servers that ODBC connects to are set up by two files, `/etc/odbc.ini` and `/etc/odbcinst.ini`. The second of these files contains the names of some libraries; check that these refer to the most up-to-date versions in `/usr/lib`.

Note that the `odbc.ini` file can contain passwords – a potential security risk. Using a private `.odbc.ini` in your home directory can reduce the hazard.

These files are often supplied with the correct settings for MySQL and PostgreSQL already coded. You can edit these files manually, or install the `unixODBC-kde` package which contains `ODBCConfig`, a graphical editor for the setup files. This package includes the `DataManager` command which generates a tree-structured display of all the data sources, databases, tables and fields that ODBC can access.

4.1.3.4 Connecting ODBC to OpenOffice

In the OpenOffice word processor or spreadsheet select

Tools → Data Sources...

then click on

New Data Source

and give your data source a new name.

Set the database type to ODBC. Now click on the button labelled with three dots and hold your breath. If everything is set up correctly a list of ODBC data sources will be displayed and you can select one of them. If you have a driver missing, OpenOffice will either crash now or in one of the next few steps. If this happens, go back and check that you have all the drivers loaded and that ODBC is set up correctly.

Now click on the ODBC tab. Enter the user name with which you log into the database – this might not be the same as your ordinary login name.

Click the Tables tab next. Choose the tables which you would like to be available to the word processor and the spreadsheet.

You can use the Queries tab to construct SQL queries – these are commands to the SQL server which tell it to choose parts of the database, sort records into order and organize them into groups. SQL can do some very useful things, including using information from one database to query another. If you want to learn SQL, the easiest way to do it is to work through the tutorials in either the PostgreSQL or MySQL packages.

Click on the **OK** button when you have set up your database connection, then press **F4** to begin using the database.

Some databases will appear to be read-only in OpenOffice – you cannot enter any data – when you would expect them to be writable. This is usually because OpenOffice needs a hidden key field to keep track of how it orders the records. Create a simple database using OpenOffice, then look at its structure with `mysql` or `psql`, and you will see the extra column.

4.1.4 Evolution

This is a new package which is a combination of appointment calendar, task list, address book and e-mail client. The address book can access remote *Lightweight Directory Access Protocol* (LDAP) servers.

4.1.5 GnuCash

Another new product, GnuCash is a double-entry bookkeeping system. At the time of writing it is perfectly usable even though there remain some areas that are incomplete.

GnuCash can import accounts in Quicken (QIF) format, keep track of an account tree with dozens of ledgers, and print some reports. It can also produce both cheques and invoices.

4.1.6 MrProject

A simple project management tool, MrProject keeps track of resources, tasks and time. It can produce Gantt charts and reports.

4.1.7 Office application compatibility

It is possible to exchange Microsoft Word documents and Excel spreadsheets between a variety of systems. OpenOffice can both import and export files in these formats. OpenOffice's own document format is itself interchangeable with the versions of OpenOffice that run on other platforms.

Databases which use dBase, LDAP and SQL are fairly easy to exchange with other systems. An address book that I made eight years ago in dBase format on an OS/2 machine is readable today with OpenOffice.

Most database software can export in *Comma Separated Value* (CSV) or *Tab Separated Value* (TSV) formats, which OpenOffice can import. Some TSV files, particularly those generated by Corel office, contain newlines in the middle of text fields. This stops the import process. TSV and CSV are plain text formats, it is fairly easy to correct the offending records with an editor such as emacs.

EXERCISES

4.2 Create a database using either PostgreSQL or MySQL.

4.3 Connect this database through ODBC to OpenOffice.

4.4 Make a table in that database listing all your friends' cars.
Include the make, model, colour, registration and owner's name.

4.5 Print a sheet of labels, one for each car, suitable for labeling pictures of the cars.

4.2 Graphical tools

Graphical tools come in two flavours – those that operate on images and those that work with vectors.

Images are stored in your computer as a list of colours to display at different points on the screen or print on a page. The words *bitmap* and *raster* are used for this kind of graphics. This works well for pictures captured from real life with scanner or camera. Images drawn with a paint program contain much sharper edges and do not take to being scaled up or down – they disintegrate into jagged edges and broken lines. Figure 4.2 shows how this happens.

Vector graphics are held in a different way. A vector graphic can contain directions such as 'Go to a point 2 inches from the top of the paper and 1 inch from the left. Draw a circle 1 inch in diameter centred here'. You can make that sort of graphic twice the size by doubling all the numbers in the command and the software that puts the graphic on the display or prints it will draw a larger circle. Because the software is drawing the graphic again from scratch, rather than manipulating an already drawn image, vector graphics can be scaled and rotated with no loss of quality.

Software such as Imagemagick can convert vector graphics into images. Doing this loses information that cannot be retrieved, which is why there are no programs that reliably translate images into vectors.

4.2.1 The Gimp

This is the GNU Image Manipulation Program – a tool for drawing or retouching images. It is a free program and can be downloaded from http://www.gimp.org/. It is also included in many major distributions. Users who have developed their graphics skills on commercial paint programs can easily transfer to Gimp.

As well as painting, Gimp has a range of effects. It can blur, sharpen, enhance and distort images. There are filters that will create mosaic tiles and obscured glass.

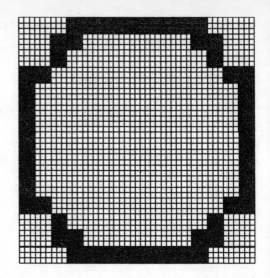

Changing the size of an image can make it become very jagged.

Changing the size of a vector graphic does not reduce its quality.

Figure 4.2 Bitmap and vector graphics

Gimp is not really suitable for drawing diagrams, its strength is as a tool for the graphic artist.

4.2.2 Vector drawing tools

Both the Applix and OpenOffice packages come with vector drawing tools. These are both extremely usable – the diagrams in this book were drawn with Applix graphics.

Both packages do the same things – you can draw lines, curves, boxes, polygons, circles and ellipses with either. Applix graphics is also integrated with the Applix word processor – you can embed a drawing in a word-processor document. OpenOffice includes a similar mechanism, graphic objects can be dragged and dropped into word-processor documents.

4.2.3 Imagemagick

This package is a collection of separate programs which manipulate images.

The display program does more than simply display an image on the screen. It also has a menu interface to many of the other programs in the package.

This package contains a program called `convert`. As well as converting images from one form to another it can turn vector graphics in PostScript format into bitmaps, insert line drawings or text captions, capture images from X-Windows and zoom images larger or smaller.

`Convert` can also apply filters. These are programs which can make an image softer or sharper and do a wide range of special effects.

One of the major strengths of Imagemagick is that it is scriptable – I will explain this in detail in a later chapter. If you need to convert several thousand images from one format to another you can write a script to automate the conversion and leave it running overnight.

Imagemagick is included in many distributions, or you can download it from `http://www.imagemagick.org/`.

4.2.4 Scanners and digital cameras

Scanners are handled under Linux by a package called *Scanner Access Now Easy* (Sane). This is not only available for Linux, but works with other operating systems as well. Sane is made up from two sets of programs:

- *Back ends* – These are the handlers for individual models of scanner.
- *Front ends* – These are the programs the operator uses to access the scanner.

Any back-end program should work with any front end.

The simplest front-end program is xscanimage. It has a convenient graphical interface and can run the scanner in a low-resolution 'preview' mode – useful to make sure that you have put the correct original right way up in the machine.

Scanimage is an alternative, text-only front-end program which can be run from a script. You can use it to build scanning into any other program. I have a simple script which works as a photocopier by scanning a document, converting scanimage's output to PostScript and sending it to the printer.

You can learn more about Sane at http://www.mostang.com/sane/.

The gPhoto package runs under Linux and gives you access to digital cameras. You can find out about it – or download it – at http://gphoto.sourceforge.net. Once again it is included in most distributions.

The gPhoto package contains two components – the graphical front end, and the camera driver library. The driver library works with over 300 models of camera and can be used with programs other than the gPhoto front end.

There is a scriptable front end for gPhoto. You can use this to trigger your camera to take pictures at specific times, or in response to events such as a door being opened.

4.3 Some other interesting applications

Finding applications for Linux is rather like browsing in a good bookshop – intriguing and unexpected things turn up all the time. For example, Linux is being used to model drug molecules, see http://www.tripos.com/ and experiment with mathematics, at http://www.wolfram.com/.

This is a selection of some of the most useful applications.

4.3.1 Astronomy

The Clear Sky Institute at http://www.clearsky institute.com distributes Elwood Downey's XEphem program, which is a star chart and an ephemeris (a program that calculates the movements of the planets).

You can download a free version of this program, or buy the full version, complete with a catalogue of 70 million stars, on CD-ROM.

Once you have entered your location on the Earth's surface – there is a handy table of cities to help – XEphem will do the rest and give you the freedom of the night sky. It can display views of the Moon and Mars, and track the satellites of Jupiter and Saturn.

Even if you only have a passing interest in astronomy this program is completely absorbing.

EXERCISE

4.6 Download the free version of XEphem, install it on a laptop if you have one. On the next clear night display the sky view for your location and try to find at least three real constellations that match what you can see on the screen.

4.3.2 Mastering CDs

The filesystem on a CD is different from that on a normal disk, because it never has to be modified during the life of the disk.

There are three main types of CD:

- Music CDs. These have a series of tracks, each containing uncompressed audio data.
- Data CDs. These usually have a single data track containing an ISO 9660 filesystem, and are also called CD-ROMs.
- HFS CDs. These are intended for Apple Macintosh computers and have a single track containing a Hierarchical File System. These can be mounted on Linux systems by setting the filesystem type to HFS. Some Linux distributions are supplied on HFS CDs.

The word 'track' when applied to a CD does not mean the same thing as a track on a hard disk. A CD track is a collection of data of any length. The CD has a *Table of Contents* (TOC) which lists the tracks on a CD, their positions and their sizes.

The original ISO 9660 standard for CD-ROMs specified that the files on them should have filenames that were eight characters, a dot and three more characters (often called '8.3 filenames'). This standard was then modified by the 'Rock Ridge' and 'Joliet' extensions, both of which allow long filenames – but in two totally incompatible ways.

You should use the Rock Ridge extension when creating a CD for use on Linux. It not only handles the long filenames but permission and ownership information as well. The Joliet extension – which is not as general – is only needed if you are creating a CD with long file names for use on Microsoft Windows.

The mkisofs program takes a filesystem tree and converts it into a single file which contains an exact image of the data to be written to the CD.

The program cdrecord then transfers the file created by mkisofs to your CD recorder – and makes the CD. You can repeat this process, known as 'burning' the CD, to make many identical CDs.

You can send the output of mkisofs directly to cdrecord by using a pipe like this

```
mkisofs /home/user/lots_of_files | cdrecord
```

which saves disk space (a CD is around 700 megabytes). Only do this is you cannot find the disk space to run mkisofs then cdrecord. If anything goes wrong with mkisofs it will stop producing output and ruin your CD.

There are several GUI interfaces you can use to make CD mastering simpler, such as xcdroast and gnometoaster. These are simple point-and-click front ends to mkisofs and cdrecord.

Read the man pages for mkisofs and cdrecord for more information.

EXERCISE

4.7 Use mkisofs to convert your /home tree into a CD image. Do you have to be logged on as root to do this? What goes wrong if you put the output file into /home? Mount the image with the loop option – read the man page for mount to see how to do this. Do the filesystems look the same? If you have access to a CD writer, make a CD from your output file. Is this CD a useful backup of your files?

4.3.3 Music and audio

As shipped, most Linux distributions come with simple audio drivers that play and record sounds.

The files on your computer that contain sounds can be in several different formats:

- Uncompressed audio. This format gives the best recording quality, equivalent to a CD, at the expense of using the largest files.
- Compressed audio, such as OggVorbis and MP3. This gives some loss of quality but much smaller files.
- Sequencer information, for example MIDI (see below). This is not strictly a recording format, but a list of which notes to play and when. The program that plays a MIDI file has to supply the sounds itself.

The *Musical Instrument Digital Interface* (MIDI) standard was originally developed as a way of connecting electronic musical instruments to one another and to computers. The MIDI interface connectors that you see on the back of electronic keyboards are high-speed serial interfaces, used to tell an instrument which notes to play, when and how long to sustain them. Linux can interface to MIDI through serial or USB ports.

MIDI files store the commands that would be sent to an instrument, and can hold information about tempo, instrument voices, and even lyrics. The MIDI Manufacturers' Association website at http://www.midi.org/ has a lot of information about MIDI.

To do more with audio you can add several packages.

The *Advanced Linux Sound Architecture* (ALSA) project http://www.alsa-project.org/ is developing improved audio drivers for Linux. These are expected to replace the current *Open Sound System* (OSS) drivers.

If you would like to compose music using Linux you can download the Rosegarden package. Its home page is at http://www.rosegardenmusic.com which has the source. Pre-compiled binaries are available from The *Center for Computer Research in Music and Acoustics* (CCRMA), which is based at Stanford University http://www-ccrma.stanford.edu. CCRMA has an extensive collection of music software. They also have their own installation tool which locates and installs packages.

Much music software runs in real time because it has to make the decision to play the next note on the correct millisecond. Running it often requires installing a specially modified kernel which can respond quickly when a task needs to be run. CCRMA have modified kernels available for download. Note that the CCRMA installer is almost the same as Debian's apt-get command. It will attempt to correct dependency problems with packages that have nothing to do with music, so you may find it simplest to add Rosegarden as the first package after installing Linux.

The Lilypond package, at http://lilypond.org/stable/, produces printed sheet music. You can transfer Rosegarden compositions to Lilypond for printing.

Linux also includes some useful sound packages which can be run from the command line:

- Sox – This is a simple converter between sound file formats which can also add some effects.
- Timidity – This is a player for MIDI files which uses pre-recorded samples of notes. It can write the results to a .wav audio file, or play it directly through the sound card.
- Playwave – A simple program to play audio files, this command is named 'play' on some older distributions.

Each distribution of Linux – sometimes each version – comes with one or more packages that can play or edit sound files. These change frequently and so I have not tried to document them here.

You can run Rosegarden on a computer that has a basic sound interface, one that does not have a built-in synthesizer. This involves compiling from source. Download the source packages, unpack them with tar (see Chapter 8) and follow the instructions. Install the ALSA drivers, build Timidity with the options

--enable-audio=alsa --enable-alsaseq

then build Rosegarden, setting the options

--without-arts --without-ladspa --without-jack

when you configure it. You can now run Timidity with the -iA option, and it will pretend to be a MIDI instrument connected to an ALSA driver.

EXERCISES

4.8 Set up your desktop to play some sounds on common events, such as opening and closing windows. Where are the files which contain the sounds kept? What happens if you play them with the `playwave` command in a shell?

4.9 Use the `sox` program to add reverberation to a .wav file. Try some other effects as well.

4.4 Games

Linux is well supplied with card games, board games, puzzles and civilization-building simulations. These function well with X-Windows, which was originally designed with work rather than play – particularly play involving fast action – in mind.

Any distribution will come with a dozen or so games of this kind. Finding out exactly what you have and how to win all of them is a good way of wasting a week or two and playing lots of really irritating background music.

Fast-action games are becoming available. They depend on an extension to X-Windows called OpenGL which connects video cards with hardware accelerators to programs, including games, that can produce high-speed moving picture output.

One of the best demonstrations of this extension is Tux Racer, available at `http://www.tuxracer.com/`, a game which involves guiding a small penguin down a ski slope, grabbing frozen herrings and trying to stay on course.

There is more information about OpenGL at `http://www.opengl.org/`, including information about video cards that work with OpenGL.

The website `http://www.linuxgames.com/` is an abundant source of downloadable games and news about new releases.

4.5 Web, mail and news

Running a browser – or any other application that makes use of the internet – on Linux is very easy. The underlying kernel takes care of the internet connection, leaving the browser to deal with the things it does best.

The World Wide Web has been seduced from its original intention – that any page should be viewable with any browser. You will from time to time come across websites that simply do not work with some browsers. There is no excuse for this – it is simply careless design. The 'Viewable With Any Browser' campaign, http://www.anybrowser.org/campaign/, is working to combat the problem of browser-specific websites. On their site you will find a design guide and some sample polite e-mails that you can send to the webmasters of troublesome sites.

4.5.1 Mozilla and Netscape

Mozilla is an open-source browser project with a website at http://www.mozilla.org/. Netscape is a commercial organization at http://www.netscape.com/. Because Mozilla is a free, open-source, project, anyone writing another browser is free to use Mozilla components in their programs. Some versions of Netscape use Mozilla components, which is the cause of some confusion between the two browsers.

Both browsers have the same features: a web browser, an e-mail program, an address book and an HTML editor.

4.5.2 Opera

This browser is a commercial product. You can download a free version at http://www.opera.com/, which pops up odd advertisements from time to time, and then buy the full version (without the adverts) online later. Opera loads web pages signif-icantly faster than other browsers.

4.5.3 Lynx

This is a text-only browser which you can install on Linux. It cannot display graphics, although it will offer to download them. To run it, type the command 'lynx' in a shell.

Because lynx is a text-only browser it can be scripted (I will explain this in a later chapter) and used as part of a larger program to archive or index websites. I recently used it to archive and cross-reference a writers' discussion site which contained 1.3 gigabytes of data in 68,000 postings.

EXERCISE

4.10 Choose a browser that includes an HTML editor. You will probably find that Mozilla is included in your distribution. Use it to construct a simple web page with some text in different styles, a picture and a table. Download a different browser and look at the same page (hint: a web page on disk has a URL that begins file: /). What is the same and what is different? What does your web page look like if you use the lynx text-only browser?

4.5.4 POP and SMTP

The two protocols normally used to transfer e-mails are *Post Office Protocol* (POP) and *Simple Mail Transfer Protocol* (SMTP). When using SMTP the computer which is sending the e-mail connects to a remote machine and pushes the e-mail through the connection. POP, on the other hand, works by connecting to a remote mail server and pulling e-mails out of it.

Most mail software uses SMTP to send and POP to receive, and ISPs are usually set up to accept SMTP connections for outgoing e-mail and POP for incoming. The *Internet Message Access Protocol* (IMAP) is an alternative to POP.

Unless you are unreasonably lucky, or spend far too much time surfing the web, the person you want to send an e-mail to is unlikely to be online at the same time as you are. The internet caters for this by using what are known as mail relays. Your ISP will have a mail relay; you send your outgoing mails to it using SMTP. The mail relay then looks up the domain the mail is addressed to. Usually it will find another relay – this time at the addressee's ISP – and hand the mail on. When your friend logs on they then collect their mail using POP or IMAP.

You can use this mechanism with Linux, or you can create your own mail server with Sendmail.

EXERCISE

4.11 Set up your chosen mail client and exchange e-mails with a friend.

4.5.5 Sendmail

This is a large and very complex program which not only delivers e-mails, but can redirect them and rewrite the mail headers to exchange mail between incompatible systems. Configuring Sendmail is a specialized task. It is normally simplest to use a configuration supplied with your distribution.

Sendmail can be set up either to send mails directly to their recipients, or to send them via a 'smart relay', another machine which passes mail on for you.

Using a smart relay, usually the SMTP server at your ISP, removes the need for your copy of Sendmail to do all the lookups involved in delivering an e-mail. The smart relay will also take over responsibility for retrying delivery if the recipient ISP's mail server goes down or cannot be reached. If you are on a dial-up connection it is usually best to use a smart relay if one is available, or send your outgoing e-mails directly to your ISP's SMTP server.

Sendmail can deal with incoming e-mails if your ISP will deliver by SMTP – not all ISPs offer this feature. If you want to make use of this, set up your firewall to accept connections on the SMTP port but, and this is vitally important, *only allow connections from IP addresses which you know belong to your ISP's mail servers*. Sendmail is normally set up to refuse to relay e-mails – it will not accept an e-mail from outside unless it is addressed to one of the users of your machine. It is possible to change this setting, for example if you want to use one machine on your LAN to forward all outgoing mail for all the other machines. Be very careful if you do this as there is a real risk of creating an open relay, a mail forwarder which will send on any e-mail presented to it.

This is an open invitation to mail spammers. They will find your machine by port scanning and then use it to send a mudslide of dubious advertisements – all of which will appear to come from you.

I will explain how to test for, and fix, an open relay in Chapter 7.

4.5.6 POP and IMAP servers

Sendmail collects incoming e-mails and puts them in the user's mailbox files in /var/spool/mail. Some mail client programs can collect their mail directly from this directory.

If you would like to use mail software that can only collect mail either via the POP or the IMAP protocols, or if you would like to set up an incoming mail server that can be used by everyone on your LAN, you can install the imap package.

This package contains both the POP and IMAP servers. Access to them is controlled by the xinetd daemon.

A daemon is a program which is always present in a system, but uses almost no resources until it is needed. Xinetd (eXtended INterNET services Daemon) is rather like a hotel porter who sits quietly out of sight watching the main doors. When a guest arrives he appears and helps them, but if an undesirable character tries to get in he turns them away. Similarly xinetd sleeps watching incoming network connections, attaches the legitimate ones to servers and rejects intrusion attempts. This makes xinetd both a router of legitimate requests and a second-stage firewall.

4.5.7 Usenet and the NNTP protocol

Network News Transfer Protocol (NNTP) is used to operate usenet newgroups. Newsgroups are discussions – either open or restricted – organized as lists of postings, which have the same general format as e-mail messages.

Imagine a usenet newsgroup as a large noticeboard with a title which describes the subjects that should be discussed there. For example the newsgroup uk.comp.os.linux is intended for discussions of Linux in the United Kingdom. Then someone comes along and pins up a note saying 'Can anyone suggest good card-game programs for Linux?' Other people seeing the note might reply with details of patience and poker games.

If you would like to participate in usenet discussions you have a choice of client programs. The one built into the Mozilla browser is suitable for a new user. You can either connect directly to a NNTP server at your ISP – simply get the name of the server from your ISP and set it in the browser's preferences. Or you can set up your own server as described in section 7.3.5.

Newsgroups are a good source of information about Linux. You will find a lot of helpful and knowledgable people taking part in the discussions and answering questions from new users. Before joining in a discussion it is a good idea to lurk – read the group without posting – for a few days. Newsgroups can also degenerate into pointless bad-tempered arguments, in which case the only thing to do is quietly move on.

05

more
powerful
features

In this chapter you will learn:

- how to use scripts to make complex operations automatic
- how to make things happen automatically at preset times
- how to use a printer with Linux
- how to run Windows software on Linux

5.1 Basic scripting (*optional*)

You should read this section if you want to know how to automate simple tasks, or if you intend to read any of the sections on programming.

The shell programs, such as bash, can take commands from script files as well as from the keyboard.

These script files should not be confused with the batch files which exist on some other operating systems. Batch files are a legacy of the practice, common in the 1960s and 1970s, of putting commands, programs and data together on decks of punched cards, piling them up into batches and leaving the computer to work its way through a batch of jobs one by one.

Script files can do much more. They can be simple lists of commands but they can also be small programs in their own right. A script can be written to make decisions and perform repeated operations automatically.

The examples in this section are text files, which you can create and edit with a text editor. Both GNOME and KDE desktop environments have built-in text editors. Do not attempt to edit script files with a word processor. Most of the time it simply will not work.

The emacs editor is more complicated but in the long term I have found it to have many more useful features. If you intend customizing your system or learning to program, it is well worth taking the time to learn to use emacs.

Emacs has a huge number of commands but initially you can get by with just three and pick the others up as you go along.

Note that because emacs runs on a large number of different computers it uses a slightly unfamiliar terminology for the keyboard. The **Ctrl** and **Shift** keys, which have been inherited by the PC keyboard from the days of the mechanical printer terminal, have the same names in emacs. The **Alt** key, which had a completely different function in the early days, is frequently referred to as *meta*, this is derived from a Greek word meaning 'to change', as it changes the meaning of a key.

The three commands you need to know are:

Ctrl-X Ctrl-S	Save the file you are editing.
Ctrl-X Ctrl-C	Exit from emacs.
Ctrl-H	Display help.

To enter **Ctrl-X Ctrl-S** hold down the **Ctrl** key and press **X** then S, while still holding **Ctrl**.

The simplest way to work with emacs is to open a terminal window, then type a command like this:

```
emacs myscript &
```

This will start emacs, which will open a new window. The file myscript will appear in the window. This will initially be blank as the file has been created with no contents. Because this leaves emacs running in background you can carry on using the terminal window to test your script.

A script normally begins with this line:

```
#!/bin/sh
```

The characters #! tell Linux that this is a script and the rest of the line is a path to the program that knows how to interpret it. The path /bin/sh is always a symbolic link to your normal shell program, usually bash. These characters must be placed right at the start of the file. There must be no spaces to the left of them or blank lines above.

The remainder of the script is then read and interpreted by the selected program.

You can experiment with a simple script like this:

- Start the emacs editor with the command:

  ```
  emacs myscript &
  ```

- Type in this simple script:

  ```
  #!/bin/sh
  # This is my first script
  ls -lrth
  ```

- Save your script to disk by entering **Ctrl-S Ctrl-X**
- Type this command

  ```
  chmod u+x myscript
  ```

  which will set the 'user executable' flag on your script. The shell will only run scripts and programs which have an executable flag set.
- Run your script by typing:

  ```
  ./myscript
  ```

You should now see the current directory displayed in reverse date order with human-readable sizes.

The second line of the script is a comment, it contains human-readable text but, because of the hash (#) at the beginning of the line, bash ignores it.

Comments are used to remind the person who wrote the script of what it is supposed to do, and how the script does it. This may not seem important at first but as the number of scripts that you have written grows into the dozens or hundreds you will find it useful to put in a few memory joggers. If you ever have to sort out a problem with a script written by someone else you will very quickly discover the value – or lack of it – of the original author's comments.

The command which runs your script begins with . / to tell the shell to look in the current directory.

If only the file name – not the full path – is given with a command the shell will look in the directories listed in the PATH environment variable. To display these type:

echo $PATH

The response should be something like this:

/usr/local/bin:/usr/bin:/bin:/home/unclebob/bin

Note that the current directory . / does not appear. When you log in your path is set to include your private binary directory, in the example /home/unclebob/bin. This directory does not automatically exist but you can create it with mkdir. The shell will then find any scripts or programs you put in this directory.

Try this with the script you have just written. Quit from emacs by entering **Ctrl-X Ctrl-S**. Then enter these commands:

mkdir bin
cp myscript bin

This will create a bin directory and copy your script into it. Now you can type

myscript

and your script will run.

Try changing to another directory and entering the same command. The new command you have added behaves in the same way regardless of which directory is current.

The shell can perform *expansion*, replacing part of a script file with something else. For example the shell will replace the string $PATH with the value of the environment variable PATH.

When you enter a shell command you can add *parameters* after the command name. The bash shell understands these parameters and hands them over to the running script. Using the same procedure as we used before, create a file called mydemo containing these commands. Be careful not to leave out any of the steps.

```
#!/bin/sh
# Demo of parameters
echo First parameter: $1
echo Second parameter: $2
```

Now run this script by typing:

```
./mydemo
./mydemo fred jim
```

In each case the shell has expanded the string $1 or $2, replacing it with the parameter. If a parameter is missing the shell replaces it with a *null string* – nothing at all.

You can use a script to repeat an operation for every file in a directory. This script,

```
#!/bin/sh
# Directory listing

for f in * ; do
    echo $f
done
```

will make a simple directory listing.

The *built-in* command 'for' makes the shell execute all the commands between the 'do' and 'done' markers once for everything it finds between the 'in' marker and the next semicolon. Because the thing between these markers is an asterisk it is expanded – replaced with a list of all the file names that match it.

Each time the commands between the 'do' and 'done' markers are executed, bash sets the variable f to one of the names on the list, working through them in order.

Expanding $f inside the markers yields the file names, one each time the commands are executed.

Now add the line

```
cksum $f
```

after the line that begins with echo. This will display the check-sum for each file.

This works properly for files, but the cksum program displays an error message for any subdirectories. You can improve the script by editing it like this:

```
#!/bin/sh

# Directory listing with checksum

for f in * ; do
    echo $f
    if [ -f $f ] ; then
        cksum $f
    fi
done
```

The built-in command if looks at the next part of the script, up to the semicolon, and tries to interpret it as meaning 'yes' or 'no'. In this case it is a built-in command which can be written as 'test' or more simply as the square brackets. The test command looks at its first argument, the -f, which means 'test for the next thing being an ordinary file'. If it is an ordinary file the 'if' command allows everything up to the 'fi' (if spelled backwards) to be executed. If not, all the commands up to the 'fi' are skipped.

The bash shell is a large and complex program. In this section I have shown you what kinds of things bash can do. There are many more features which you can look up in the man and info pages for bash.

5.2 Using cron

Cron is a program which executes in *background* all the time Linux is running. It is used to run programs and scripts at pro-grammed times, even if there is no user logged on. Cron wakes up every minute and looks in one or more crontab files to see if it has anything to do. When it has run all the required programs it goes back to sleep so that it stops consuming resources for another minute.

There are two sorts of crontab files. The system crontab which is in /etc/crontab is owned by the system and is used to run various housekeeping operations which are part of Linux itself or installed software packages. User crontabs are in the /var/spool/cron directory. Ordinary users are allowed to use the crontab command to create and edit these files.

The format of both `crontab` files is similar. This is a typical system `crontab`:

```
SHELL=/bin/bash
PATH=/sbin:/bin:/usr/sbin:/usr/bin
MAILTO=root
HOME=/

# run-parts
01 * * * * root run-parts /etc/cron.hourly
02 4 * * * root run-parts /etc/cron.daily
22 4 * * 0 root run-parts /etc/cron.weekly
42 4 1 * * root run-parts /etc/cron.monthly
```

The first part of the file sets up a series of variables which provide the environment for the running commands. Note that this file contains comment lines beginning with hash.

The second part of the file contains the list of commands to run. At the start of each line are five fields, each of which can be a number or an asterisk. These fields, in order, correspond to:

- Minutes
- Hours
- Day of month
- Month
- Day of week. 0 or 7 is Sunday, 1 is Monday and so on.

When cron runs it looks at the fields of each line in each `crontab`. Fields containing numbers must match clock time, fields containing asterisks are ignored.

Instead of numbers you can use lists. Putting 0,15,30,45 in the minutes field, for example, will run a command on the quarter hours. The full range of formats which you can use is listed on the manual page for `crontab`. Type

```
man 5 crontab
```

to see it.

In the example table the pattern

```
01 * * * *
```

has a number one (ignore the leading zero) in the minutes field and asterisks everywhere else. This will match clock time at one minute past each hour. A command associated with this will run every hour at one minute past the hour.

In the same way the line beginning

```
42 4 1 * *
```

will run at 04:42 am on the first of every month.

The field after the day of week is the user name with which `cron` will execute the command. The rest of the line is the command and its parameters. When the time to execute a command comes around, `cron` in effect logs on a session with the user name and gives it the rest of the line as if it had been typed at the keyboard.

The user name field does not exist in user `crontab` files. Instead the user name is taken from the owner of the file, and the command starts immediately after the day of the week.

You can create your own `crontab` files with the `crontab` command. To edit or create a `crontab` first choose the editor you would like to use, for example emacs, and enter this command

```
export EDITOR=emacs
```

then run `crontab` with this option

```
crontab -e
```

There will be a short delay and your chosen editor will start up. If you have a `crontab` it will appear in the editor; if not, the command will make a blank `crontab`.

You can look at your `crontab` by typing

```
crontab -l
```

Ignore the control information that appears at the beginning of the file.

Your `crontab` can be deleted with

```
crontab -r
```

This does not give you a chance to change your mind, so use it with care.

If your computer is not running at a time when `cron` should execute a daily, weekly or monthly command the `anacron` program will notice that an operation has been missed when the computer next starts up, and will run the command at once.

If the command prints any messages `cron` will e-mail them to the owner of the `crontab`. This can be a nuisance, particularly if the command runs frequently. The solution to this is to redirect the output of the command to /dev/null. This device is a 'black hole', anything that goes into it is lost for ever, nothing comes out of it.

For example if you set up a crontab entry like this to play a sound every fifteen minutes, a simple chiming clock,

```
0,15,30,45 * * * * playwave /usr/share/sounds/startup3.wav
```

you may find that the playwave command outputs a message which gets e-mailed back to you.

Adding

```
>/dev/null 2>/&1
```

to the end of the command will solve this problem by discarding the output from playwave.

5.3 Printing

Linux, in common with many other UNIX-like systems, uses print queues to organize work for printers.

Printing is controlled either by the lpd program, or on newer systems by the *Common UNIX Printing System* (CUPS). These are started automatically when Linux starts.

Most distributions now have a graphical tool for setting up printers, although no two are alike. You will need to know the make and model of your printer and which port it is plugged into. Once you have set up your printer it is a good idea to print a test page to check, among other things, that you have selected the correct paper size.

From the user's point of view lpd and CUPS are compatible – any command that worked on an older system with lpd will work on a current one with CUPS. CUPS can do more than lpd – it can rotate the output, print multiple pages on one sheet, add pretty formatting and even mark your printout TOP SECRET.

To learn more about CUPS simply use a browser to look at the URL http://localhost:631. This page is generated interally by CUPS. From this page you can browse the manuals, or log in as root and change the settings.

The lpr command is used to print files. It either takes the name of one or more files to print, or the data to print can be sent to its standard input.

For example the command

```
lpr fred.txt
```

will print the file `fred.txt`, and

```
ls -l | lpr
```

will print the output of the `ls` command.

This command places the data to be printed in a print queue. The queue is organized as a series of jobs, each job prints one or more files, each time you run `lpr` it creates one job. You can look at the contents of the queue with the `lpq` command.

You can cancel a job with the `lprm` command. As an ordinary user you can only cancel your own jobs. If you log in as root you can cancel any job.

Most distributions include graphical front ends for these commands. You will normally find that you can print a file by dragging it to the printer, display the queue in a window and cancel jobs by clicking on them.

If you are using `lpd` you can log in as root and use the `lpc` command, or `lpadmin` and its relatives if you are using CUPS, to control your printers. You can abort print jobs, stop and start printers, close a queue so that new jobs cannot be added to it and change the order in which jobs will be printed.

Each printer has one or more filters associated with it. A filter is a program or script which processes the files to be printed before sending them on to the printer.

Some very simple printers can only print text. The filters used with these printers do little more than pass on the text from the print job to the printer.

Printers with more capabilities need to be able to print lines, circles, curves, bitmap graphics and text in a variety of fonts.

The easiest way of doing this is to have the various programs, such as graphics packages and word processors, produce their output in a standard format. The filter then converts this format into something that a particular printer can understand.

Many printers, particularly those manufactured by Hewlett-Packard, use a format called *Printer Control Language* (PCL).

Alternatively there are printers that use PostScript format. This format was developed by Adobe Systems Inc. Unlike many proprietary formats this one is well documented, both a reference manual and a tutorial have been published by Adobe. PostScript is a plain text format and can be edited with an ordinary text editor. An example of PostScript is shown in Figure 5.1.

PostScript is a vector format. If a PostScript file contains, for example, a circle drawn one inch in diameter, two inches from the top of the page and three from the left margin, the PostScript file describes it by listing those measurements.

Some, not all, variants of PCL use bitmap formats for graphics. The circle would be described by a list of dots to print.

The advantage of vector formats is that they are very easily scaled and rotated. The mpage command can take a PostScript format file and edit it so that, for example, several pages of the original document are printed on one sheet of paper.

Many Linux systems use PostScript or plain text as the standard formats for printer output. All programs that send output to the printer use one of these two formats.

When you print a file Linux passes it through a filter. The simplest type of filter will recognize plain text or PostScript by looking at the first few characters of the file and then do whatever processing is needed to prepare that file for the printer. Some systems, including CUPS, have a magic filter. This lets you send a file in any one of the formats it knows about to the printer. The filter will automatically work out what format the file is in and print it correctly.

You can send print jobs over the network to printers on other computers. The computer with the printer is called a print server, and the printer is known as a remote printer or network printer, as opposed to a local printer which is connected to the machine on which you are working. Linux lets you use these types of print servers:

- Another Linux or UNIX machine.
- A computer running Microsoft Windows.
- A Novell server.
- A printer with a built-in JetDirect server.

Once a remote printer has been set up, any program can use it in exactly the same way as it would use a printer directly connected to the computer.

A remote printer has a print queue on the local machine. When a program sends a job to a remote printer the job is first put into

```
%! Postscript

%! Body
newpath
144 144 72 0 360 arc
stroke

%! Head
newpath
144 252 36 0 360 arc
stroke

%! Beak
newpath
124 236 moveto
144 216 lineto
164 236 lineto
stroke

%! Eyes
newpath
124 260 10 0 360 arc
stroke

newpath
164 260 10 0 360 arc
stroke

%! Feet
newpath
100 110 moveto
120  70 lineto
140 110 lineto
closepath

148 110 moveto
168  70 lineto
188 110 lineto
closepath

stroke

showpage
```

Figure 5.1 PostScript

the local queue. The lpd or CUPS program then sends the job over the net to the print server. The print server may have its own queues, and your job may next spend some time in the server's queue, waiting to get onto the printer. You can use the lpq command to look at the status of your job while it is in the server's queue.

When you set up a remote printer you should set the printer type on the server to the real type of the printer. On the machines which make use of the printer set the type to 'PostScript printer' or 'Raw print queue'. This way jobs which are sent across the network are in PostScript format, which is a reliable standard, and any changes to the printer settings only need to be made in one place, on the server.

CUPS prefers the *Internet Printing Protocol* (IPP) but is compatible with the older lpd protocol. There is a problem with some distributions at the moment which set up the lpd protocol with no filters, so remote systems can only print plain text. The fix for this is documented in the man page for cups-lpd. To print to an lpd server from a machine running CUPS set up a 'Raw print queue' on the client.

When you are experimenting with the settings on a program that produces printer output it is useful to see on the screen what would be printed without actually printing anything. Not only does this save paper, it is much quicker as well.

Almost all the filters which convert PostScript to the commands needed to operate a particular printer use a program called ghostscript internally. This program converts PostScript into images of the pages to print, then outputs those images in a variety of formats.

Ghostscript can be run directly from the shell by typing the gs command. I do not recommend this, ghostscript's commands are not easy to understand or to use. It is much better to use one of the wrappers, gv or ggv, which give ghostscript a simple point-and-click interface. Set the application to print to a file, then look at the file with ghostscript.

One possible problem with printing is a mismatch between the paper size of the document being printed and the paper size chosen when the printer was set up. If this happens the printing will appear moved up or down on the page, and a few lines at the top or bottom will be chopped off. Newer versions of the filters attempt to correct this problem automatically.

The Portable Document Format (PDF) standard is similar to PostScript. Documents created to this standard can be viewed on many different browsers. Adobe, creators of the standard, also make a program called the Acrobat Reader available for download from `http://www.adobe.com/`. The command `ps2pdf` will convert PostScript files to PDF format.

EXERCISE

5.1 Print the list of filesystems mounted on your computer.

5.4 Emulating other environments (*optional*)

There are some applications which have only been released for operating systems other than Linux. You can run these on Linux by using an emulator.

There are two kinds of emulators. The first kind emulates the computer itself and runs a guest operating system, such as Microsoft Windows, on the emulated computer. You can then use this guest system to run applications which were designed for it. This method uses a real copy of the guest operating system which has the advantage of running the applications in exactly the environment they expect. It has the disadvantage that a licensed copy of the guest operating system must be bought and paid for.

The open-source emulator Dosemu (`http://www.dosemu.org/`) emulates a simple PC and will run MS-DOS. It will also run Freedos (`http://www.freedos.org/`), an open-source free replacement.

The commercial emulator VMware (`http://www.vmware.com/`) will run most versions of Microsoft Windows, and several other systems. This package has the remarkable ability to absorb a crash of the guest operating system. It has a `redo` log which allows you to rewind time, restoring the virtual machine's hard disk to its uncorrupted state before the crash.

The second kind of emulator does not require a guest operating system. Instead it attempts to duplicate the thousands of points of connection between application programs and the operating system. These are collectively known as the *Application Programming Interface* (API). The Wine emulator (`http://www.winehq.org/`), which is free, works in this way. At the time of writing it is capable of emulating, not quite perfectly, most versions of Microsoft Windows.

There is one Linux distribution called Linspire (http://www. linspire.com) which is built around an enhanced version of Wine. This distribution offers a familiar desktop, and will run common applications such as Word, Excel and Outlook. It offers the stability and reliability of Linux while allowing you to run familiar applications. It can also run Linux applications at the same time.

5.4.1 Using Dosemu

From the Dosemu website download the two tar archives containing the emulator and a copy of Freedos, and the README file. These will be on the 'stable releases' page under 'binaries'. The exact installation sequence can vary from one release to another, so it is worth checking the README file for the current version.

Dosemu can run either in its own window – type ./xdosemu to start it – or it can use an ordinary terminal window if you type ./dosemu. With the KDE and GNOME desktops you can also create a desktop object to start Dosemu by clicking with the mouse.

The file mydos/dosemu/conf/dosemu.conf contains a list of options which can be changed using a text editor.

If you are installing Dosemu on a laptop which uses an external USB floppy you can change the line which reads

```
$_floppy_a ='threeinch'
```

to read

```
$_floppy_a ='threeinch:/dev/sda'
```

which will access the first USB disk as the floppy. If you have other USB or SCSI disks the name of your floppy may be different. The names of the SCSI and USB disks are /dev/sda, /dev/sdb, /dev/sdc and so on.

5.4.2 Using VMware

This program can be downloaded from http://www. vmware.com. You will need to obtain a licence to use it. Short-term, evaluation licences are normally available free of charge, or a permanent licence can be bought online. There is also a version of this program available on CD-ROM.

5.4.3 Using the Wine emulator

At the time of writing this emulator is still under development and is not perfectly stable.

It works well enough to be useful and runs an impressive array of applications.

Wine can be installed from a `.rpm` package, or a `tar` archive. It creates a directory which is a replacement for the C:\ drive and populates it with appropriate subdirectories. The configuration file can be common or each user can have their own copy in the directory `.wine` under their home directory. It tells Wine where to look for all its files and directories, which devices it can access and what options to set.

The directory which is used as C:\ is normally common to all users. Because of this it is also read-only. You can make a private copy of this directory in your own home directory, and alter your copy of the configuration file if you want to have a C:\ that you can write to.

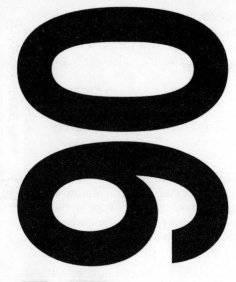

06

linux and networking

In this chapter you will learn:

- to understand TCP/IP concepts and technology
- how to connect a Linux machine to the internet
- how to solve network problems
- how to share files with other machines

Linux, in common with other UNIX-like systems, has networking built into the kernel. It also has a range of network test and analysis tools which are so comprehensive that I have regularly used them to resolve problems on networks which use other operating systems.

6.1 TCP/IP basics

When computers communicate across a network they use a *protocol*, a set of rules for how messages are to be structured, or more often several protocols stacked one inside the other. Linux can communicate using a variety of protocols, the most widely used of these is the 'Transfer Control Protocol – Internet Protocol' almost always referred to as TCP/IP.

The TCP/IP protocol, and its descendants, is described by an extensive list of standards. These are described in a set of documents known as the 'Requests for Comments' or RFCs. The title is something of a misnomer. By the time a document becomes a published RFC it has been adopted as a standard. With a few notable exceptions the RFCs define the official and correct forms of all the major protocols. The RFCs are listed online at

http://www.faqs.org

with duplicate mirror copies on many other sites.

Computers connected to a network communicate by some form of signalling, such as electrical impulses carried on a cable. Ethernet and serial links are examples of this sort of network. Alternatively the computers may get in touch by flashes of light sent down an optical fibre or, using the new Bluetooth standard, by radio. Many other forms of communication have been used. There is an infamous spoof RFC (Number 1149) dated 1st April 1990, which describes the problems involved in routing TCP/IP via carrier pigeons.

How the components of TCP/IP interconnect is described by the *Open Systems Interconnection* (OSI) standard. This standard is concise to the point of woeful obscurity.

Because TCP/IP will work over any sort of network it is designed to conceal the details of the hardware from the programs that use it.

The hardware in your computer which connects to a network may have an address permanently burned into it during manufacture. For example the address of an Ethernet card is six, eight-bit, binary numbers. The Ethernet address of the card in my computer is 00:60:08:30:8F:91. The interface which it uses to connect to the outside world is made with a different type of hardware and doesn't have an address at all.

To make all interfaces work in the same way TCP/IP assigns an *IP address* to each interface. The IP stands for Internet Protocol. This is written in a different form, called dotted decimal notation. An address written in dotted decimal notation looks like this:

192.168.0.2

The four parts are numbers in the range 0 to 255.

An IP address is assigned when an interface is installed and is always in the same form. It can change if a computer is moved from one place on a network to another. A hardware address, if it exists at all, is assigned when the interface is manufactured and never changes. The format of a hardware address depends on the type of hardware being used.

The Internet Protocol address is so called because, except for some special ranges of addresses, a message sent to an IP address will be delivered to the correct computer even if it has to travel half way around the world through a dozen intermediate machines to get there.

The software in your computer which handles messages, and the software that forwards them, deals in datagrams, blocks of information sent from one program to another. It puts headers onto the datagrams, a process similar to putting a letter into an envelope and writing on an address, so that they can be delivered correctly.

Datagrams can be up to 65,535 characters in length – about the size of an average short story – although very long datagrams are rarely used. To avoid the practical problems involved in moving around very large blocks of data, datagrams are often fragmented, the fragments being sent as separate packets across the network.

Programs can, if they choose, communicate by sending and receiving these messages directly, making use of the *User Datagram Protocol* (UDP). This protocol is fast but it contains no error checking. If datagrams arrive in the wrong order, or some are lost in transmission, the receiving machine does not know that there has been an error.

Most of the traffic over the internet is handled by TCP, the *Transfer Control Protocol*. TCP uses similar packets to communicate but adds error checking and correction. Once a TCP connection has been established between two computers it will either work correctly or announce the fact that it has failed. Programs using TCP do not have to worry about errors in the received data itself.

Most of the remaining protocols, such as e-mail and the *HyperText Transfer Protocol* (HTTP) are constructed using TCP. These protocols simply set out what sort of data is sent, and how it is laid out, leaving the mechanics of transferring it to TCP.

When you communicate with another computer over the internet, for example when you look at a website, it is much more convenient to use the remote machine's name, rather than its IP address. Your computer can translate a name into an address, and back again, in two ways.

Firstly there is the file /etc/hosts. This contains a list of IP addresses and the name or names – one machine may have several aliases – of the computers that go with them. This is part of /etc/hosts on one of my computers:

```
127.0.0.1     localhost localhost.localdomain
192.168.0.2   falstaff
192.168.0.3   oberon
192.168.0.4   puck
192.168.0.7   titania
192.168.0.10  portia
```

Note that the first entry is for the loopback address. Datagrams sent to this address simply bounce back to the computer they came from. The loopback address is one way in which two programs on the same computer can communicate through a form of TCP/IP. The other addresses are the computers on the Local Area Network or LAN. These addresses are in a range which is reserved for private networks. Computers outside the LAN do not appear in this file.

The second way of converting between names and addresses is to use the *Domain Name Server* (DNS). A DNS is a program which provides information about computers on its section of a network, queries other servers and answers queries from application programs.

You can set up your own DNS or you can use one on another machine.

Setting up your own DNS is very simple. If you install the name-server package, called 'bind', and a standard set of configuration files known as the 'caching nameserver', your DNS will configure itself automatically.

A DNS works by querying one or more of the 'root nameservers', a small number of computers which supervise the DNS lookup mechanism. From them it learns which nameservers to query for all other possible requests.

The DNS has to be able to find the root servers before it can begin working, but it has to be working before it can find anything – initially it is in the same state as a person wondering who to phone to ask for the number of directory enquiries. It uses a hints file, which is part of the DNS package, that contains the IP addresses of the root servers. These addresses very rarely change and so, if you operate your own DNS, you need only update this file at intervals of weeks or months. The file /etc/named.conf will tell you where, on your machine, to look for this file.

One small network, connected up by one set of cables, is called a *segment*. All the computers connected to a segment can directly communicate with each other. A larger network may be made up of many segments, right up to the millions of segments that make up the internet itself. These segments are connected together by machines called *routers* which handle datagrams in the same way that sorting offices handle letters.

A Linux machine can become a router if it has two or more network interfaces. You can make a machine work as a router by switching on forwarding, setting up the routing table and optionally making rules with the iptables command.

Forwarding is turned on by this command

```
echo 1 >/proc/sys/net/ipv4/ip_forward
```

which writes figure 1 to the appropriate part of the /proc filesystem.

The routing table tells Linux which interface to use to send out datagrams for particular destinations. You can examine the routing table by logging in as root and typing the route command. You can also use the route command to change the table. With most current distributions there are GUI tools to manipulate the routes which are much easier to use.

A routing table is a list of rules describing how to send out packets.

A typical example is shown in Figure 6.1. Each packet is tested against every rule in order until a match is found.

The first two routes send datagrams to single computers. The next directs datagrams to a subnet beginning at 192.168.37.0 through the interface vmnet1. The Genmask field indicates that this rule applies to a range of addresses. There then follows a rule for another subnet with a larger address range. The rule beginning 127.0.0.0 sends datagrams to the loopback device. An address in this range only communicates with another program on the same computer. The final rule covers every possible address and catches all remaining datagrams. This route goes to 'the rest of the internet' and goes via a gateway (explained below) at Demon Internet, my service provider.

Masks are used to tell Linux if a route applies to a range of addresses or a single machine. How a mask works is shown in Figure 6.2.

You can write subnet addresses in dotted decimal notation. The example uses the subnet address 5.17.192.0. The binary representation of the address is shown under the numbers. A mask is written in the same way; in the example the mask is 255.255.192.0. At the bottom of the page is an address that might, or might not, be in the required range. Putting the subnet address and the mask together gives a pattern in which the binary digits are marked as 'Must be a 1', 'Must be a 0' or 'Don't Care'. Binary digits that have the value 1 in the mask mark where binary digits in the subnet address matter, zeroes in the mask indicate digits that don't matter. Test that pattern against the unknown address, if all the binary digits except the ones marked 'Don't Care' match, the address is part of the subnet – in the example it is. This subnet has the address range 5.17.192.0 to 5.17.207.255 – all the addresses in this range are part of the subnet described by the subnet address and the mask.

Some rules refer to a *gateway*, another computer that forwards packets to a subnet or the whole of the internet. The Linux kernel will arrange that packets for that destination are sent to the gateway, which then forwards them.

When you are using a network, such as Ethernet, which uses hardware addresses, each packet sent out by one interface must be labelled with the hardware address of the machine or machines that the packet is going to. There are three sorts of hardware address. Unicast addresses go to one particular machine, packets with the broadcast address are received by every machine on the

```
Kernel IP routing table
Destination      Gateway           Genmask          Flags Metric Ref    Use Iface
demon-du.demon.  *                 255.255.255.255  UH    0      0        0 ppp0
falstaff         *                 255.255.255.255  UH    0      0        0 eth0
192.168.37.0     *                 255.255.255.0    U     0      0        0 vmnet1
192.168.0.0      *                 255.255.255.0    U     0      0        0 eth0
127.0.0.0        *                 255.0.0.0        U     0      0        0 lo
default          demon-du.demon.   0.0.0.0          UG    0      0        0 ppp0
```

Figure 6.1 A routing table

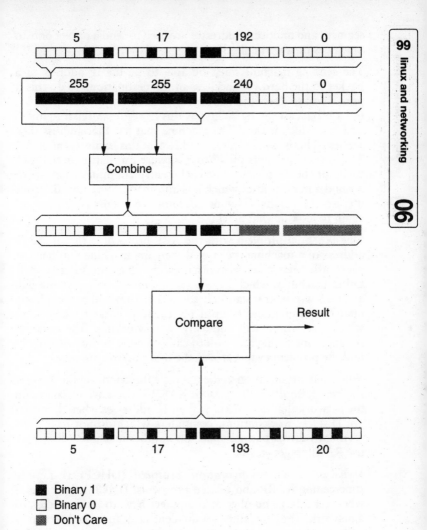

- ■ Binary 1
- □ Binary 0
- ▓ Don't Care

Figure 6.2 How a netmask works

segment and multicast addresses are used to send a packet only to machines on a particular list.

The sending machine must be able to tie the IP address of a packet to the hardware address of the destination. To do this it uses *Address Resolution Protocol* (ARP). The sender first puts out a broadcast saying 'Who has this IP address? Tell it to my IP address, which is this.' The machine that has that address then replies, 'This is my IP address and I am at this hardware address.' This transaction puts the IP-to-hardware translation in the ARP cache of the originator. The cache entry continues to exist for around a minute, after which it is automatically removed. While it exists the sending machine does not need to use ARP protocol again to look up that machine.

One potential problem with the ARP protocol is that if the IP address of a machine is changed then any machine that has not previously been in contact with it will be able to connect at once. Other machines, which have been in contact, will have the old, and now wrong, translation in the cache. They will be completely unable to communicate until the cache is correct again, after which everything will suddenly start working. The delay is roughly long enough for you to call someone for advice, only to find the problem evaporates as the other person answers.

You can use translation in the opposite direction, via the *Reverse Address Resolution Protocol* or RARP, if you have machines on the network that do not know their IP addresses when they start up. Diskless workstations, computers which do not have their own hard drives but use space on another machine's disk, may use RARP to get started.

Dynamic Host Configuration Protocol (DHCP) is rapidly superceding RARP and related protocols. DHCP is very useful wherever a large number of computers have to be connected to a network. They can all be set up identically, then the hostnames and IP addresses are handed out automatically by a DHCP server. These can either be set up manually in advance, or the DHCP daemon can generate IP addresses automatically when it finds a new machine on the network.

When you install Linux with networking it sets up the forwarding rules so that, if forwarding is turned on, every datagram that can be forwarded is forwarded. This may not be what you want, particularly if you intend the machine to act as a firewall to protect itself, or a subnet, from unauthorized access.

At the time of writing the graphical configuration tools for firewalls are rather limited in what they can do. Manually editing /etc/sysconfig/iptables, which contains the configuration, gives you access to all the features.

In section 7.4.2 I will explain how to set up a simple firewall.

EXERCISE

6.1 Use the route and ifconfig commands to find out how the networking is set up on your machine. Examine the ARP cache with the arp command.

6.2 Internet access

A connection to the internet is the same as any other network interface – once it is connected.

Setting up your computer so that it will establish a connection and identify itself is, with modern distributions, almost completely automatic. On RedHat for example you can select

    System Settings → Network

then click on the 'New' icon and follow the instructions. This will work with most *Internet Service Providers* (ISPs), or at least with those that conform to the agreed standards for TCP/IP and PPP. If an ISP insists that you must use their special software to connect they are probably not complying, and it is time to find another ISP.

With *always on* connections, such as ADSL or connections made through a LAN, choose automatic configuration. If this does not work supply the IP address and netmask. Set the default route to the gateway address. Your provider or LAN administrator can tell you the correct settings.

Most home computers connect to the internet using a *modem*, short for *modulator/demodulator*, a device that converts data into tones that can be sent along a telephone line and converts them back at the other end. Modems have evolved over the past few decades. Originally they were boxes larger than a modern computer, then they shrank down to the size of paperback books and recently they have become single chips inside the computer.

For many years modems were either connected to, or behaved like, the ordinary serial interfaces on a computer. They could be told to dial, hang up the phone, change their settings and adjust the internal loudspeaker by sending them simple commands in plain text. These commands were known as the *Hayes* or AT command set, after the Hayes Corporation which introduced them, and the letters AT which came at the start of most commands.

Unfortunately, in the past few years there has been a trend towards manufacturers producing incomplete modems or 'win-modems' which require extensive external software to make them work, then not releasing the required software or documentation for Linux. The situation is improving, Linux drivers are becoming available for an increasing range of these devices. The website http://www.linmodems.org is a useful starting point for finding suitable drivers.

You can set up your modem in two ways. Either you can set it to dial on demand, when you try to access any address that is outside your own computer or local area network, or you can start and stop the connection manually.

If you choose demand dialling you can set the idle and holdoff times. When you stop using the internet for the number of seconds set as the idle time Linux will hang up the call, and then, after the holdoff time, dial a new call if you start using it again. Choosing the idle and holdoff times carefully can save you money on your phone bill if you are charged for the number of seconds you stay on the line. Usually, idle times of between 60 and 180 seconds and a holdoff of 5 to 10 seconds are appropriate.

When the modem connects to your ISP Linux must identify you to a computer at the ISP's end of the line. There are two common ways of doing this. Script authentication is used if the ISP expects your machine to send the user name and password as plain text. Point to Point Protocol authentication is more secure and reliable but not all ISPs work this way. Your ISP *should* be able to tell you which they use. Unfortunately, experience teaches that not all ISPs' support staff have the required technical knowledge.

Fortunately, there is a very simple way of sorting out the problem. As root, type this command

```
minicom -s
```

then, when the terminal emulation comes up, press **Escape**.

You should see the minicom terminal emulator start up and try to initialize your modem. You may hear some clicking.

Now type

```
atz
```

and press **Return**. If all is well with your modem it will reset itself and either reply OK or 0.

Next type atdt followed by your ISP's access number and press **Return**. Your modem will dial and the word CONNECT will appear.

If the next thing to come up is a readable prompt such as

Login:

you may need script authentication, try both. If you see a line of random characters including lots of curly brackets, select PPP authentication.

EXERCISE

.2 Set up an internet connection on your machine.

6.3 Troubleshooting TCP/IP

Linux comes with an assortment of tools for diagnosing network problems. To use these you will need to understand how TCP/IP works, as explained in the previous section.

6.3.1 Ping

Ping is the simplest of the network diagnostic tools. It sends packets to a remote machine and displays the replies. It is a very quick and useful way of checking that two machines are in communication.

You can specify several options to ping. The flood option, -f, sends packets as quickly as possible. This is a good way of performing a full-load test on a network segment. It should be used with caution, and never across the public internet. Your ISP will not thank you for performing a full-load test on their machines (which are already heavily loaded), however interesting the results.

One common problem which you can diagnose with ping is the incorrectly set *Maximum Transmission Unit* (MTU) – the amount of data the interface will send in one packet. The symptoms of this are a connection which works correctly for ping but fails when transferring significant amounts of data.

Log in as root and use the ifconfig command to find the current MTU for the interface which is suffering errors. Use ping to test the connection but set the -s option to make the size of the packets about twice the MTU. If ping now reports errors you can reduce the MTU with `ifconfig` – the other machines on the same segment will probably have the correct value set. Once you have a working connection you can make the change permanent by changing the network settings using a GUI tool.

EXERCISE

6.3 Pick a suitably distant machine – for example a web server in another country. Ping it and make a note of the round-trip time.

6.3.2 `Traceroute` and `xmtr`

`Traceroute`, which you can run as root, finds out how packets reach a distant computer. It works by sending packets similar to those used by `ping`, but it sets the *Time To Live* (TTL) field in the header to a small value, initially one. Each router that forwards this packet reduces the TTL by one. When the TTL reaches zero the router sends a 'time exceeded' error packet back to the sender.

The 'time exceeded' mechanism was originally intended to deal with the problem of circular routes on the internet. These shouldn't exist – they are a symptom of corrupted routing tables – but they still occasionally happen, even in the best regulated of networks. Packets which get into a circular route would end up orbiting endlessly around three or more routers. Because each time a packet is forwarded it sacrifices one unit from its TTL these packets are ultimately removed from the network.

`Traceroute` sends out a packet with a TTL of one, and waits for a response. It sends three packets, then increases the TTL to two and tries again. It goes on increasing the TTL until it either finds the destination or reaches some maximum value, usually 30.

For each value of TTL it displays the identity of the computer that has responded and the time in milliseconds taken by each packet to make the round trip.

`Traceroute` is useful but not completely reliable as not all operating systems send back the correct error packets. The official documentation for `traceroute` actually contains the phrase 'God only knows what's going on' describing the behaviour of one machine.

Typical output from `traceroute` is shown in Figure 6.3. This shows the route between my computer in England and a web server in Hong Kong. Long-distance routes like this vary from

```
[root@falstaff /root]# traceroute www.conferencehongkong.com
traceroute to www.conferencehongkong.com (212.67.208.138), 30 hops max, 38 byte packets
 1  anchor-du-24.access.demon.net (195.173.57.24)  94.647 ms  75.800 ms  69.731 ms
 2  anchor-core-1-fxp3.router.demon.net (195.173.57.251)  79.547 ms  77.329 ms  79.650 ms
 3  anchor-core-11-242.router.demon.net (194.159.187.18)  79.774 ms  75.503 ms  69.746 ms
 4  anchor-border-1-4-0-2-549.router.demon.net (194.159.187.1)  79.577 ms  84.308 ms  79.727 ms
 5  ge3-0.br1.lnd6.gbb.uk.uu.net (195.66.224.16)  89.630 ms  73.687 ms  79.772 ms
 6  srp4-0.cr1.lnd6.gbb.uu.net (158.43.194.233)  79.548 ms  76.003 ms  79.529 ms
 7  pos11-0-0.gw4.nth1.gbb.uk.uu.net (158.43.253.41)  79.749 ms  77.662 ms  77.322 ms
 8  fe4-0-0.gw6.NTH1.Gbb.uk.uu.net (158.43.156.69)  89.651 ms  96.395 ms  79.685 ms
 9  webinte01-gw.pipex.net (158.43.112.246)  819.774 ms  86.284 ms  79.758 ms
10  212.67.210.234 (212.67.210.234)  103.185 ms  104.862 ms  119.734 ms
11  212.67.208.138 (212.67.208.138)  99.730 ms  137.526 ms  99.766 ms
```

Figure 6.3 Traceroute output

time to time as routers are added, removed and shut down temporarily for maintenance.

The xmtr program does the same things as traceroute, but has a convenient graphical interface.

EXERCISE

6.4 Find the route that the packets took in the previous exercise.

6.3.3 Tcpdump and ethereal

Tcpdump, and its GUI equivalent ethereal, let you look at what is going on inside Linux's networking. You can run either of these by logging in as root.

Tcpdump produces text output and is adequate for analysing simple problems. Its advantage is that its output can be displayed on basic devices, such as terminals connected to serial ports.

If you want to see the contents of the packets translated into readable text and have an X-Windows display available, use ethereal. There are many display options: Ethereal can decode or show as numbers most parts of a packet. It also has a very useful ability to follow a TCP stream. Select a TCP packet on the display and choose 'Follow TCP Stream' from the Tools menu, and it will display all the captured traffic on that stream. It uses different colours and columns to differentiate the two different directions of transfer, and it can show the contents of the packets as either text or hexadecimal. It allows you to examine packets not only in ASCII but also in EBCDIC (Extended Binary Coded Decimal Interchange Code), an alternative character code which is less common.

You can also capture packets with ethereal, put them in a file and analyse them later.

Both tcpdump and ethereal have packet filters which you can use to pick out just those parts of the network traffic that are relevant to the problem you are solving. You can filter by protocol, source and destination addresses and with ethereal by almost any field within the packet header.

Type in

man ethereal

to see how to set up the display filter. This controls which of the captured packets will appear on the display. There is a separate capture filter which restricts the packets that are actually captured by the program. This filter is identical in tcpdump and ethereal – it is the same library software that does both. Type

man tcpdump

for instructions.

When capturing packets these programs will switch the interface into promiscuous mode. Despite its startling name this is quite innocent. Normally a network interface card uses simple filters to screen out network traffic that is bound for other addresses. Telling it to go into promiscuous mode simply turns the filter off, so it will receive every packet that is available on the network.

EXERCISE

6.5 Look at the packets transferred when you call up a web page. Why might some come from different servers?

6.3.4 Route and name resolution

The programs in the previous sections will tell you what is happening on your network. The route command can sometimes tell you why.

The most worrying type of networking problem is the complete failure of a new network to communicate, either internally or with the outside world.

If this happens the best thing to do is first to turn off the firewall – about the only time I will advise you to do this – and see what happens. If the network surges into life one or more of your firewall rules is wrong. If not, you probably have a problem with either routing or name resolution. Do not do this with a connection to the public internet in place.

I am going to handle these together because routing and resolution interact in several non-obvious ways. What may seem to be a resolution problem often turns out to be routing, and vice versa.

Resolution – the process of turning the names of computers into IP addresses and back again – can be done in several ways. The file /etc/resolv.conf tells Linux how to set about resolving names. There is a man page for this file that describes its format. This file can contain the addresses of one or more nameservers.

The route command, along with several others, uses name resolution in order to include the names of other machines in its output. To do this it has to be able to contact at least one of the nameservers – which it won't be able to do if routing is incorrectly set. But to work out what is incorrect about the routing you need to use the route command.

The way out of this problem is to use the -n option, which makes the command display the routes as numbers rather than trying to translate them. If you type the route command with no parameters and it appears to freeze with only part of its output on the screen, try killing it with **Ctrl-C** and typing

```
route -n
```

instead. If this works, your machine cannot reach a nameserver, or it is a nameserver and it can't contact the outside world.

Once you can see the output from route the next step is to make sure that you have:

- A loopback route.
- A route to every subnet of your local area network.
- If your local net is connected to the outside world, a default route that goes somewhere suitable, such as a firewall machine or a connection to the internet.

Now check that you can ping at least one other machine by entering its IP address, not its name. Use tcpdump or ethereal to see what packets are sent out by your computer.

6.3.5 ARP

You can investigate problems with address resolution by using the arp command.

Your computer keeps a list of the translations between the hardware addresses of other computers on the same subnet, and their IP addresses in a cache. Type arp with no parameters to see the current contents of the cache. There are three common ways in which the address resolution mechanism can go wrong.

- An old entry can be left in the cache after a machine has either changed addresses or been replaced.
- Duplicate hardware addresses are very rare as the interface card manufacturers assign the addresses uniquely. Mistakes can happen, particularly if there is any way of changing the address of a card after manufacture.
- Missing entries – machines on the network which do not show up in the cache.

The symptom of an address resolution problem is usually one or more completely unreachable machines. Dropped connections – sudden loss of contact between machines – are rarer but possible.

You can solve this kind of problem by making a list of the machines on the subnet together with their IP and hardware addresses. The ifconfig command – either log in as root or type /sbin/ifconfig – will show you these. Its output should look something like this:

```
Link encap:Ethernet HWaddr 00:00:E2:45:91:3B
inet addr:192.168.0.7 Bcast:192.168.255.255
  Mask:255.255.0.0
UP BROADCAST RUNNING MULTICAST MTU:1500 Metric:1
RX packets:26277 errors:0 dropped:0 overruns:0
  frame:0
TX packets:36325 errors:0 dropped:0 overruns:0
  carrier:0
collisions:2222 txqueuelen:100
RX bytes:2459697 (2.3 Mb) TX bytes:30228324 (28.8
  Mb)
Interrupt:11 Base address:0x3000 Memory:f4100000-
  f4100038
```

Each interface should have an IP address (inet addr) and hardware address (HWaddr) which is unique – not shared with any other machine. The Mask and BROADCAST values must be the same for all machines on one subnet.

If, having made sure these settings are correct, the network is still not working, the next step is to use the route command to make sure that packets intended for the machine that is giving trouble are routed to the correct interface and, where relevant, are sent via the right gateway machine.

You can use tcpdump or ethereal at this stage to see what is actually happening on the network.

Beyond this you should begin to suspect hardware problems – this is where the little LEDs (Light-Emitting Diodes) on the back of network cards and on hubs become very useful. If generating a ping from the failed machine produces no response in the lights, but the software thinks a packet has been sent, you probably have a failure.

6.4 File sharing

The *Network File System* (NFS) is frequently used to share files between Linux machines. NFS uses the *Remote Procedure Call* (RPC) protocol to communicate across any network. The RPC protocol, developed by Sun Microsystems, sits on top of the IP layer of TCP/IP and lets a program on one computer call a library routine on another.

RPC effectively conceals the differences between the hardware of the two computers. The NFS layer uses this to make a filesystem on one computer appear on another. Differences between the systems are absorbed by the NFS and RPC layers and, subject to a few restrictions, there is very little difference between a filesystem mounted on a local disk drive and one mounted over NFS.

Files are exported by an NFS server. This is a machine which has the nfs daemon programs installed.

Each line in the file /etc/exports on the server describes a part of the local filesystem to export, some options and a rule describing the computers that are allowed to use the exported filesystem.

For example you can create (log in as root) a directory called /sharedfiles and use the command

```
chmod a+w /sharedfiles
```

to make it writable by any user. Then, as an ordinary user, copy a few files into it.

Next edit /etc/exports (this time as root again) to add the line

```
/sharedfiles *
```

which will share this directory to any machine that asks for it.

The NFS export daemon has to find out about the change. The command

```
exportfs -r
```

will tell the daemon. This command has to be entered as root. If you began with either no /etc/exports or an empty file, the daemon will not be running. In this case type (as root)

```
/etc/rc.d/init.d/nfs start
```

then wait for everything to come up.

You have now set up a simple NFS server and can test it by using the showmount command. Type

```
showmount -e localhost
```

as root to see the filesystems exported by this machine. This command should give the same results on any computer on the network if you enter the server's name in place of 'localhost'.

Now you can go to another machine in the same network and mount the exported filesystem. As root create a directory for the mount point and mount the exported filesystem on it. For this example I am going to call the server 'titania'. Type

```
mkdir /imported
mount titania:/sharedfiles /imported
```

and the shared filesystem will be mounted. You can check this by typing

```
ls /imported
```

and then look at the data in the files as well.

There are two common reasons for this to fail. Firstly there are simple typing errors. The error messages NFS gives can be misleading here. The second reason is that some NFS servers will not allow access if they cannot find the client machine either in their /etc/hosts file or by looking it up on a nameserver.

An NFS mount can be added to /etc/fstab, just like a mount of a local disk. It is possible to mount NFS filesystems when the client machine starts and unmount them again at shutdown.

If an NFS server shuts down and restarts it is quite common for clients to keep running – some NFS operations will keep retrying for a long time. This is not without its problems – sometimes it can be difficult to unmount a filesystem which is mounted on a server which has been shut down. Automount is a partial solution to this. I will explain how to set it up in the next section.

NFS works very well with diskless machines. These are computers which do not have their own disk drives but make use of disks on other machines over the network. When you switch on a diskless machine it uses a protocol such as DHCP to find out its own IP address, loads its operating system over the network and starts it. Then it mounts its root filesystem using NFS.

If the diskless machine is a diskless workstation – it has a screen and keyboard – it can either have its own password file in the mounted filesystem or it can use the *Network Information Service* (NIS) to pick up the list of users, passwords and users' home directories.

When NIS is combined with NFS any number of workstations on a network can be made to behave identically. A user can sit down at any workstation, log in using their user name and password and find themselves in exactly the same home directory. This works very well for some purposes, such as graphics, where there is a lot of user interaction. It goes wrong where the bulk of users are running disk-intensive applications as all the disk traffic has to cross a local area network which rapidly becomes overloaded.

Diskless Linux machines are comparatively rare. Much more common is the machine which runs from a local disk drive and uses NFS to access a pool of shared files.

NIS allocates user names and the numbers that correspond to them in one place. When computers with their own disk drives and password files are added to a network which is already using NIS, the result is a descent into anarchy.

For example, let us assume that a user called 'Castor' is known to NIS, and has the user number 523. Castor can log in anywhere in the network and find his files under /home/castor – and nobody else has access to them. This works until someone adds another machine to the system. This computer has its own disk drive on which there is a freshly installed copy of Linux. Its owner, who has root access to his own machine, creates a user called 'Pollux' with user number 523. Instantly he has full access to all of Castor's files.

The only real solution to this is to do one thing or the other. Either use NIS on every machine or none.

The situation is worse if the owner of the new machine logs in as root – now he can access every file on the server. To control this problem the server can be set up to perform 'root_squash' – it 'squashes' all requests that seem to come from root on the client machine into an innocuous user who has very few access rights.

6.5 Using automount

The automount package bypasses the need to mount and unmount some filesystems. It sits watching a selection of mount points and, when a user program tries to access one of them, it mounts a filesystem. When the user program stops accessing that filesystem automount waits for a preset time and unmounts it again.

This is particularly useful for removable disks such as CD-ROMs and floppies, and for NFS filesystems.

You can set up automount by logging in as root and creating map files in /etc. You can create a list of maps in auto.master, which looks like this:

```
# Format of this file:
# mountpoint map options
# For details of the format look at autofs(8).
/oberon /etc/auto.oberon              --timeout 120
/puck /etc/auto.puck                  --timeout 120
```

Each line of this file associates a mount point with a map file. The map file contains a list of the filesystems that can be mounted as subdirectories of that mount point. This is the contents of /etc/auto.oberon:

```
root           -ro,soft     oberon:/
maint          -ro,soft     oberon:/maint
cdrom          -ro,soft     oberon:/cdrom
dos            -ro,soft     oberon:/dos
backup         -rw,soft     oberon:/backup
external       -rw,soft     oberon:/external
```

The computer called oberon exports the filesystems /, /maint, /cdrom, /dos, /backup and /external. Note that exporting /, the root filesystem, is *not* a good idea in general, although there were special reasons for doing it in this case.

Once automount is running it takes over control of the /oberon mount point and something like this appears in the mount list – type mount with no parameters to see it:

```
automount(pid424) on /oberon type autofs
   (rw,fd=5,pgrp=424,minproto=2,maxproto=3)
```

When you run a program that refers to /oberon/dos automount will look in the map file and mount oberon:/dos over the network on /oberon/dos. If there are no accesses to this filesystem for 120 seconds – the timeout value in auto.master – automount will unmount it again.

Automount is almost invisible, applications normally do not know that it is there. However if you look at /oberon when nothing is mounted, the directory will be empty.

There is also a problem with some versions of automount if it is not shut down cleanly. It can leave mount points mounted and think they are still mounted even if the computer is rebooted. The quick solution to this is to find the stray mount points with mount and unmount them explicitly with umount.

6.6 Interworking with Microsoft systems

Small office networks which use Microsoft Windows and related operating systems – such as IBM's OS/2 – share files and printers through a network protocol called *Server Message Block* (SMB). This protocol is not quite standard, it exists in several slightly different versions.

SMB can be carried over TCP/IP, or over Ethernet without the TCP/IP headers using a protocol called *NetBIOS Extended User Interface* (NETBEUI). NETBEUI is not compatible with IP routing – to get the best out of your network you may want to replace it with TCP/IP.

There are both client and server programs for running NFS file sharing on Microsoft systems. At the time of writing, very few of these were genuinely free – almost all were expensive commercial packages.

If you want to run graphical Linux programs from a computer which uses Microsoft Windows you can use the Cygwin package which can be downloaded from http://www.cygwin.com/ or one of its mirror sites. This package creates a UNIX-like environment on Microsoft Windows. It includes a version of X-Windows – you can use it to connect over your LAN to a Linux machine and run X applications. To install it simply start the setup program directly from the website, select the base and XFree86 packages and let it run. If you need to install this package on more than one computer, or if your connection to the internet is less than perfect you may find it easier to download the package by using ncftp or a similar program on a Linux machine and then installing Cygwin from a hard-disk directory.

The Samba suite of programs for Linux lets you share files between computers running Linux and Microsoft systems.

The Samba server itself shares files and printers to the network. It is controlled by the samba.conf file, which lists all the shares together with security and setup information. If you are setting up a network on which some users will want to run Microsoft Windows, but all users need to share files, you can install a Linux machine as file and print server – and as firewall if the network is to be connected to the internet. This way you can take advantage of the low cost and reliability of Linux while still letting everyone on the network use any application software they choose.

Setting up and maintaining the Samba server can be done by editing the samba.conf file with a text editor such as emacs. You will find that it is much easier to use the *Samba Web Administration Tool* (SWAT). This package presents the samba.conf file as a series of web pages. These pages contain simple forms which you can fill in with the details of users, file and printer shares, and security information. SWAT then edits samba.conf automatically.

SWAT is a web server – it provides pages to browsers. It can run side by side with a conventional server on the same machine because it uses a non-standard port number. For example if your server is called ourserver, and it runs both a conventional web server and SWAT, the URL of the index page of the conventional server will be

http://ourserver

and SWAT will be at

http://ourserver:901

which can be bookmarked or linked to in the conventional way.

If you cannot see the SWAT server at this address there are three things to check. First check that the file /sys2/etc /xinetd.d/swat has been set up correctly. Make sure that the 'only_from' field is set to show the computer you are using to access SWAT, and that the 'disable' field is set to 'no'.

The Samba suite includes two programs to access files shared by SMB servers. The smbclient command will attach to a server then send and receive files. It uses text commands, similar to the commands used by the ftp program. Smbclient can also send popup messages to other machines.

Alternatively you can mount a filesystem which is exported by another system on a Linux machine.

Log in as root and create a mount point unless one already exists.

For example:

```
mkdirhier /smb/ourserver
```

Then you can mount the SMB filesystem with a command like this:

```
smbmount //ourserver/docs /smb/ourserver/ -o
                    username=bob,password=hush
```

If you now look at /smb/ourserver you will find the files in the share docs on the server ourserver appear in that directory. SMB mounts can be placed in /etc/fstab in the usual way.

If you do not get a connection to a Windows system at the first attempt the cause of the trouble is probably one of these things:

- A host name that cannot be resolved by the DNS or by reference to /etc/hosts.
- The wrong hostname set for the server.
- The workgroup names are different on the Linux and Microsoft systems.
- The 'master' parameters are incorrectly set. It is usually better if you can let the Linux machine become master. If not, turn all the master parameters off and let a Windows machine take over.
- A password is null – the user simply pressed **Return** without typing anything. This does not always stop Samba working but it can be capricious: it can stop one machine from accessing shares then have no effect on another.
- The iptables (firewall) setting is such that the SMB packets aren't getting through.
- The security parameter is set incorrectly. It should normally be 'user'.
- The encryption parameter should normally be set to 'yes', unless you have an older version of Windows that does not handle password encryption.

Once you have an SMB network up and running the next step is to exchange some files between Linux and Windows machines. Bitmapped images present no problems – the file formats are identical. Adobe PDF files are similarly compatible, as are documents in PostScript format. Some vector graphics formats are also compatible.

Files of plain text are not perfectly compatible between Linux and Windows, although the discrepancy rarely matters. The difference derives from the printer terminals used up to the end of the 1970s. Many models of these used a mechanical carriage, which moved one position to the right when a character was printed and was returned to the left-hand edge of the paper by sending the control character 'Carriage Return'. Moving all the way back across the width of the paper took longer than printing one character, so it became common practice to send 'Carriage Return' followed by 'Line Feed' which stepped the paper onto the next line. The carriage could then complete its homeward journey while the paper was advancing. This was absorbed into the format of a text file, the end of a line was marked by the 'Carriage Return – Line Feed' pair.

UNIX took a different turning and used the 'Line Feed' character as 'New Line'. This standard was carried on into Linux.

To convert a text file from the Linux/UNIX format to the one used by MS-DOS and Windows a 'Carriage Return' is added before each 'New Line' and to convert the other way the 'Carriage Return' characters are removed. You can do these conversions with the commands dos2unix and unix2dos. These commands have man pages. To make a simple conversion from Windows to Linux formats type a command like this:

```
dos2unix <dosfile >linuxfile
```

The reverse conversion is similar.

Word-processor and spreadsheet files are not as readily exchanged between different programs. There are historical reasons why different word processors, and even different revisions of the same package, are incompatible. The situation is now improving – the StarOffice package is able to read and write a large number of formats used by other programs. Certainly almost all the file formats which are commonly exchanged over the internet can be understood, and most of them generated by StarOffice. OpenOffice, which is a free version of StarOffice, has similar capabilities.

When sharing printers between Linux and Windows systems it is safe to treat every Linux printer as if it used PostScript. Set the printer type on the Windows machine to any printer (such as the Apple LaserWriter) which itself uses PostScript. In the opposite direction, when a Linux machine uses a printer on a Windows server, set the printer type to match the type of the printer which is actually connected to the server.

The basic format of a CD-ROM, as described in the ISO 9660 standard, is the same for both Linux and Microsoft systems. The extensions which allow long file names and Linux/UNIX file types are not identical, but you can create CD-ROMs with both the Joliet metadata for use by Microsoft systems and the *System Use Sharing Protocol* (SUSP) records for Linux and UNIX machines. You can read a CD-ROM created in this way on either system.

6.7 Interworking with classical UNIX

Linux interworks with classical UNIX and UNIX-like systems almost perfectly. Sun Microsystems' Solaris, Hewlett-Packard's HP-UX and similar desktop systems can act as NFS and X-Windows servers and clients. My personal experience is that, subject to the problems of integrating NIS and non-NIS networks described in an earlier section, this kind of interworking requires very little setting up – simply plug in the network cables and start sharing.

There are a number of UNIX-like operating systems, such as OS/9, supplied by Radisys (formerly Microware), which use both X-Windows and NFS. These systems are normally used for special applications, such as extremely critical real-time systems.

NFS shares files to individual computers, to ranges of IP addresses or to netgroups. It assumes that the other computers on the network are telling the truth about their identities – it cannot prevent someone adding a new computer to the network and setting it up to pretend to be a legitimate client.

This does not matter if all the computers on the network are under the control of a system manager and individual users cannot log in as root.

Files of plain text are compatible across all varieties of Linux, UNIX and similar systems – a text file edited on a Linux machine will look exactly the same on a Sun. Script files, such as bash scripts, are normally compatible between all systems.

The executable binary files of programs are always specific to one type of processor, often to one version of an operating system. Archive files, in formats such as such as tar, zip and tgz, are almost always compatible. When you unpack an archive to extract the files inside it you automatically recover the full name, ownership and permissions of every file. You can make an archive file and copy it onto a disk in a format – such as the one used by MS-DOS – which does not have long filenames, ownerships or permissions. Even if you then transfer it to another machine you will find that it unpacks correctly.

Removable disks, formatted in Ext2 or Ext3 formats, are compatible across all varieties of Linux. They are not usually compatible with UNIX systems.

An archive made with the tar program (described later) which contains all the files needed to create a particular program or collection of programs, is often referred to as a tarball. You will often find new programs available for download as tarballs. When you download one you can unpack it and inside you will find some script files which will convert the program into a binary for your machine. These scripts are very intelligent. They can work out what sort of computer you have and what operating system you are running, then adjust the program they are creating to suit.

6.8 Interworking with other common systems

There are many other types of computer system in use. Linux can communicate with them in two ways. It can always use standard protocols such as NFS, X-Windows and SMB if the other system can do the same.

Alternatively some other protocols, developed for particular systems, can be used with Linux. These are a few examples:

- The Netatalk package lets you use Apple's AppleTalk protocol to communicate with Macintosh computers.
- Mars is a package that communicates with Novell NetWare clients.
- The DecNet protocol, developed by Digital Equipment Corporation, now part of Compaq, is now built into the kernel.

6.9 Telnet, rsh and ssh

If you want to enter CLI commands into another machine across the network you can use these three protocols.

Telnet is a very simple protocol which connects the keyboard and display of one machine across the network to a shell running on another machine. To use it type

```
telnet hostname
```

and you will either see the login prompt for the remote machine or an error message.

Telnet is hideously insecure – it sends passwords across the net with no encryption at all. That is why most Linux systems are set up to reject all telnet connection attempts. You can enable telnet if you have a really good reason to need it by editing the file /etc/xinetd.d/telnet or /etc/inetd.conf on older systems.

Despite its insecurity telnet is very useful on smaller, secure networks that cannot be accessed from the outside world because it is a very convenient way of issuing a few commands to a machine that you cannot conveniently get at in any other way. My experience has been that setting up a telnet daemon on an embedded processor – one buried inside a piece of equipment – has often been a very quick and easy way of setting it up and fixing any problems.

The *Remote Shell* or rsh command runs a command on a remote machine and connects up the standard input, output and error streams through the network. You can redirect the input, output and error streams of rsh and they will behave exactly as if the command on the remote machine were executing on the local one. Rsh has to be enabled in the same way as telnet before using it and the /etc/hosts.equiv file on the remote machine has to contain the name of the local machine.

The command

```
rsh remotehost ls
```

will log into the host remotehost and take a directory listing, which will come up on your screen.

The real power of rsh is that it can pass across the network any sort of data that can be put in a stream. For example you can use rsh to run the scanimage command on another machine. This will operate the remote machine's scanner and send the scanned image to standard output. Rsh will then divert standard output over the network to the local machine, where you can redirect it.

If you have a remote machine with a scanner

```
rsh othermachine scanimage | display -
```

will scan the document in othermachine's scanner, then re-direct the scanned image to the display command and display it on the local machine's screen.

Ssh is a much less vulnerable replacement for both `telnet` and `rsh`. It should be used wherever possible. It uses secure encrypted communication and public-key authentication, which makes it proof against most intrusion attempts.

07

network management and servers

In this chapter you will learn:

- about the different network protocols
- how to use servers and clients
- how to make a network secure
- what a firewall is and how to create one
- how to deal with various kinds of attack
- when you may need a cache and how to create one

7.1 PPP

The *Point to Point Protocol* (PPP) is used to carry TCP/IP over serial lines – such as your modem connection to the internet. PPP has replaced the earlier *Serial Line Internet Protocol*, which is now effectively obsolete.

You can use the Point to Point Protocol Daemon program, pppd, to set up and control PPP lines. The various GUI tools for configuring, starting and stopping PPP connections either send commands to pppd or edit configuration files that it uses.

A PPP connection is a network segment with two interfaces – one at each end – each of which has an IP address. The PPP daemon can be told the addresses to use through its command line parameters, or it can learn them by querying the daemon at the other end of the line.

Pppd is a very versatile program. You can use it to dial up a connection to a remote machine, manage a connection between two machines which are permanently connected by a cable or accept incoming calls.

When you use pppd to dial into another system, such as your ISP, it first calls the chat command to issue commands to your modem. These commands do any setting up you choose, then tell it to dial the call. When the modem at the far end answers, chat can send your user name and password.

Alternatively the remote system may start using PPP at once. Pppd can then authenticate itself by sending 'secrets' – user name and password – as part of the PPP protocol. The *Password Authentication Protocol* (PAP) is the more common, though less secure way of doing this. *Challenge Handshake Authentication Protocol* (CHAP) is more secure as it uses a reasonably strong encryption to conceal the password.

When you use pppd to make a connection to an ISP it can ask the ISP for the IP addresses of their first two DNS machines.

Because pppd is so powerful, and can accept a large number of options it is almost always run from a script, rather than from the keyboard. The scripts which operate it are in the directory /etc/sysconfig/network-scripts. For each ppp interface that you have set up there is a file called ifcfg-pppn where n is the interface number, starting with ppp0 for the first one. If the interface uses chat to dial the call there will be a chat-pppn file as well. You will normally use the GUI tools to edit these files.

Because pppd has so many options you will usually find an area in which you can enter any option – look at the pppd man page to see what options are available.

One very useful option is 'demand'. This makes pppd only dial when there is something to send, and disconnect again when the link is not being used. The 'idle' and 'holdoff' options let you adjust exactly when it will dial and hang up.

The 'debug' option makes pppd send a lot of information about its negotiations with the remote machine to the system log. You can either read them in /var/log/messages, or edit /etc/syslog.conf to redirect them to a file or to the system console. The xconsole program lets you read console messages on a graphical screen, or you can read them directly on the first text screen – press **Ctrl-Alt-F1** to see it.

7.2 PLIP

The *Parallel Line Internet Protocol* (PLIP) is a way of connecting two computers together through their parallel printer ports. This is often faster than using the serial port. The PLIP driver is normally a kernel module which is loaded automatically when the interface is set up with ifconfig.

Older versions of the driver will only work if parallel port interrupts are turned on. Use this command:

```
echo 7 >/proc/parport/0/irq
```

substituting a different value if the irq of your parallel port is not 7.

The command

```
ifconfig plip0 192.168.100.0
```

will configure the interface. You can substitute another IP address if it is more convenient.

PLIP works by connecting five data output pins of one computer to five status inputs of another, and vice versa. You can make your own cable to do this – the instructions are in a comment in the source of the driver – or you can buy a laplink cable.

You can either write a few lines of script to set up the interface directly, or create an ifcfg-plip0 file with an editor. A PLIP interface can be treated almost exactly as if it were an Ethernet port. Configuring it by setting its IP address is enough to start it operating. Next create a route to the IP address of the remote machine, or to a subnet that is reached by routing through it, setting the gateway device to plip0.

PLIP is not commonly used – in most cases it is simpler to add an Ethernet interface than to set up PLIP. Its major virtue is that it works without installing extra hardware, and so it is sometimes a good way of installing Linux onto difficult machines which have neither a CD-ROM nor a network interface that can be used by the installation process.

7.3 Linux servers and clients

This section tells you about the server and client programs for a variety of other protocols. You may not need to use all of these – some are for specialized purposes.

7.3.1 File Transfer Protocol (FTP)

FTP, older than HTTP, is a standard, if rather clumsy, way of moving files from one machine to another. You can set up an FTP server to distribute files to other machines on your local network, or to collect files from other machines.

An FTP transfer requires two programs – a client and a server. Both of these are provided with Linux distributions. The *Washington University FTP Daemon* (wu-ftpd) is commonly used as the server.

When you set up a connection to an FTP server your client program authenticates itself by supplying a user name and password. The FTP server checks the user name and password that the client presents against its list of users, in exactly the same way that they are checked when you log in at that machine's keyboard, or by telnet. Once logged in you have precisely the same access rights to the same files as you would have with a normal login.

If you would like to make files available from your FTP server to anyone who comes along over the network you can add anonymous FTP to do this. When a client connection supplies 'anonymous' or 'ftp' as the user name the FTP server will look for a user called 'ftp' in /etc/passwd. If this user and a corresponding home directory are set up the user is allowed to log in with *anything* as password – what they enter can be recorded in the system log. The log entry looks like this:

```
ANONYMOUS FTP LOGIN FROM titania [127.0.0.1], fruitbat@
```

A user from titania (in fact this is the same machine, so the loop-back IP address has been recorded) logged in using the incomplete e-mail address `fruitbat@` as password.

Once logged in, anonymous clients are then given access to a directory tree, usually /home/ftp or /var/ftp, which you can populate with any files you would like to give out. Make sure that these files are read-only, at least to the anonymous users.

Most browsers have an FTP client built in. When you click on a link which begins ftp:// the browser will automatically make an anonymous login, using a password which you can set as part of your browser's options.

The wu-ftpd server can archive and compress files before sending them. Some clients such as ncftp can take advantage of this to transfer whole directories very quickly.

The basic ftp client is simply called ftp. To start it enter this command

```
ftp hostname
```

and it will connect to the remote host. It will then ask you for your user name and password. You can enter a real user name, 'ftp' or 'anonymous'.

It will then give you a prompt like this:

```
ftp>
```

and you can enter ftp commands. The commands you will need most often are:

get filename	Get a file from the remote machine.
mget pattern	Get all files that match pattern.
put filename	Send a file to the remote machine.
cd	Change to a different remote directory.
quit	End the session.

The mget command lets you retrieve lists of files, for example

```
mget *.jpg
```

will retrieve all the JPEG images on the remote machine. To retrieve directory trees use the server's ability to convert them into `tar` archives. For example, if there is a directory tree called `newfiles` on the server, retrieving `newfiles.tar` will tell the server to send you an archive containing everything in that tree. You can then unpack the archive with the `tar` command, which will be explained in Chapter 8.

FTP transfers can be made in either active or passive mode. Active-mode transfers involve the server making a new connection to the client for the data files. This has some performance advantages, but is often blocked by firewalls. If you set the `-p` option on the command line when you start `ftp` it will use passive mode – all connections are initiated from the client side.

FTP makes a distinction between text and binary transfers. When transferring a text file it will convert between the standard 'newline' character and the convention on your local machine. For Linux and UNIX machines this conversion does nothing.

The file `.netrc` can be a useful time-saver if you have to log in to many FTP sites regularly. It can also be a hideous hole in your security if it is misused. It contains a list of remote machines and for each the username and password with which to log in, and some commands to execute once the session is open. Once you have `.netrc` set up you can connect to a remote machine and the `ftp` client program will log you in then execute the commands. If you want to do something regularly, such as receiving or sending a day's worth of data or updating a website, `.netrc` can automate this for you. Unfortunately, to use `.netrc` you have to put your password for the remote system into the file without encryption – and with default settings this file can be more widely read than an advertisement in *The Times*. To limit the damage this can do `ftp` will report an error if this file is readable by other users, forcing you to protect it.

FTP transfers can easily be controlled by scripts, particularly if the `.netrc` file is in place. Automating routine file transfers and making file transfers part of other programs can cut down on the number of manual operations needed each day and make your system run more smoothly.

7.3.2 Trivial File Transfer Protocol (TFTP)

This protocol is a simplified version of FTP with no authentication. Its main use is with diskless machines which use TFTP to load the kernel over the network. For this sort of use it has one enormous advantage, it is so simple that it can easily be built into the machine's *bootstrap* program. The protocol itself is so totally insecure that you should never use it on a machine that can be accessed over the public internet unless you use a firewall or xinetd, or set up your /etc/hosts.allow and /etc/hosts.deny files to deny access from outside your LAN.

You can install TFTP as two separate programs – the client called tftp and the server daemon tftpd. The daemon, as supplied, is turned off for security reasons. To turn it on you can edit /etc/xinetd.d/tftp. Change 'disable' to 'no' and choose values for server_args (see below) which will make the daemon safe. In this example I have created a user called tftp with the adduser command and given this name to the daemon with the -u option. I have also used the -s option to set the server up to treat /tftpboot as its root directory. This is the relevant part of /etc/xinetd.d/tftp.

```
service tftp
{
        socket_type     = dgram
        protocol        = udp
        wait            = yes
        user            = root
        server          = /usr/sbin/in.tftpd
        server_args     = -s /tftpboot -u tftp
        disable         = no
        per_source      = 11
        cps             = 100 2
}
```

Once you have edited and saved this file use the killall command to signal xinetd. Type this command:

```
killall -HUP xinetd
```

This sends the SIGHUP signal to xinetd, prompting it to re-examine its configuration files.

One problem with tftpd begins when you change one or more configuration files, issue the killall, and nothing changes. This is because the tftpd server persists – after it has been used it sits in memory for about fifteen minutes waiting for another request. This makes sense if it is being used to bootstrap a roomful of computers on Monday morning. It saves the over-head involved in loading a fresh copy of the server for each request. Unfortunately it does not notice that its options have changed until it is unloaded and loaded again. Use the command

```
killall in.tftpd
```

to unload the daemon. It will then be loaded again with the new options when the next request is received.

You can use the `tftp` command for testing the server – enter

```
tftp localhost
```

to connect to the daemon and transfer files in either direction.

7.3.3 HyperText Transfer Protocol (HTTP)

HTTP is the protocol that transfers pages from web servers to browsers.

There are several HTTP servers available for Linux. The most often encountered is Apache. Use of this package has grown so rapidly in the past few years that it is now estimated to be running on more than half the servers on the web. You can learn more about Apache from the Apache foundation; `http://www.apache.org/` is their website.

Apache is very easy to set up. Installed from the distribution it sets up a trivial empty website, with a page which congratulates you on having set up your own web server. To start the server you can use the command

```
/etc/rc.d/init.d/httpd start
```

as root. Once your server is set up you can adjust the `init` files (this is explained in Chapter 9) to start the server automatically when the system is brought up.

You can now start adding content. Look in the file `/etc /httpd/conf/httpd.conf` for the 'DocumentRoot' line. This will tell you where Apache looks for the files that make up the website. For example it could be `/var/www/html`. Take a look around in the directory above this one. You will find these directories:

- `cgi-bin` – This contains 'Dynamic Content', pages which are generated by a program whenever a browser asks for the page. The *Common Gateway Interface* (CGI) is a standard way of writing and using these programs.

- error – In here are the pages which the server hands out when there is an error, such as a browser asking for a page that does not exist.
- html – This is your website. Make sure there is an index.html page in here which can be given out as your home page.
- icons – There are lots of icons in here which you can use in your pages.
- manual – This directory contains the instructions for Apache, starting with an index.html file.

Edit a simple page with any HTML editor – or by hand if you know HTML – and put it in the html directory with the filename index.html. Then start a browser such as Mozilla and enter localhost as the URL. You should see the page.

Dynamic content is generated by programs, normally kept in the cgi-bin directory, which generate the entire content of the page, including headers, when they are run.

The headers can be reduced down to one line,

```
Content-type: text/html
```

which warns the browser that HTML is coming. This *must* be followed by a blank line to mark the end of the headers.

The rest of the output from the program is the content of the page.

This is a trivial bash script which generates very simple dynamic content – a page containing the date and time:

```
#!/bin/bash

# CGI compatible real time clock

echo "Content-type: text/html"
echo
echo "<HTML>"
echo "<head>"
echo "<title>CGI Clock</title>"
echo "</head>"
echo "<body>"
echo "Time now:<br>"
date
echo "</body>"
echo "</HTML>"
```

When you run this script it generates a page containing the date and time. Put this script into the file

`/var/www/cgi-bin/clock`

and use this command

`chmod a+x /var/www/cgi-bin/clock`

to make it executable. It will add a dynamic page with the URL `http://localhost/cgi-bin/clock`. Click 'refresh' on your browser to see the time update.

Apache has many options, all of them are explained in the online documentation.

When a CGI page is called up by a browser the script or program that generates it is run on the server. It is no different from any other program and it can do everything that an ordinary program can do, including reading and writing files. This is how a great many guest book and discussion board applications work.

A large quantity of information about the request from the browser is passed in the environment variables to a CGI program. The program can use some or all of this to modify the contents of the page it hands out. It is possible to use this to make the page content depend on which browser is being used. Please don't, unless you can guarantee that a usable page is given out to browsers you can't identify.

This is very important if your website is to be used for electronic commerce. Customers who are faced with a web page that tells them that you won't fit in with their choice of browser will go to your competitors as fast as a mouse up a drainpipe.

The basic idea of the World Wide Web – that any page should be visible on any browser – has been compromised by the number of web pages that are 'Optimized for browser X'. Only too frequently this means the page takes advantage of some specific features, or in the worst case bugs, in browser X. Net surfers using browser Y get annoyed because they can't read the page. This need not happen – it is often easier to make a page work for any browser than debug browser-specific code.

Web-enabled appliances, electronic devices which can be monitored and controlled from a browser, work in the same way. The CGI scripts which are run when the user clicks on a link either get status from the electronics, operate controls, or do both. For this sort of application, which commonly uses an embedded processor, there are much simpler servers available. For example the thttpd (Trivial Hyper Text Transfer Protocol Daemon) server, available from http://www.acme.com/, is about one-eighth the size of Apache but contains all the features needed for a web-enabled appliance.

If you are setting up an intranet server for an organization, or a server that will be available over the public internet, you can use Apache almost as distributed. It is advisable to read the manual carefully, particularly if you intend to write your own CGI code, as it is possible to introduce security holes with carelessly written CGIs.

7.3.4 Domain Name Server (DNS)

The named daemon which you can use as a DNS was described in Chapter 6.

In its simplest form it either connects to another server, or finds the root servers, and translates publicly available names and IP addresses.

You can set up a private DNS which will resolve the names of the computers within your organization. If you are running a large intranet with 20 or more computers this is possibly the best way to go.

There are three approaches to name serving on intranets:

- Circulate a new version of /etc/hosts every time the network changes. This is time consuming but simple. It is useful on very small networks that rarely change.
- Use NIS to circulate the hosts file. This is easy to set up but does not have all the features of a DNS.
- Set up your own DNS. This is versatile, allows servers in different parts of the network to cooperate and can make your computers visible to the public internet if that is what you want to do. Setting up a DNS is not difficult, but there is a lot of documentation to read. The Administrator Reference Manual which shows you how to set up a fully functional DNS can be downloaded from http://www.nominum. com/ in PDF format.

Alternatively there is a script called host2dns which can be downloaded as part of the YADDAS (*Yet Another*

DNS Database Awk Script) package from `http://www.digitalanswers.org/yaddas`. This will convert the `/etc/hosts` file on one machine into the configuration files needed for the DNS. On current distributions you will also find GUI tools for setting up a DNS.

The format of the configuration files is somewhat confusing, mainly for historical reasons to do with the way in which the earlier *Advanced Research Projects Agency* (ARPA) network, the precursor of the internet, handled addresses. For a time the DNS system had to handle both ARPA and internet addressing schemes, and it still carries some baggage in the form of disorganized file formats.

7.3.5 Network News Transfer Protocol (NNTP)

This is the protocol used to organize `usenet` discussion groups. Messages posted to `usenet` are in the same format as e-mails. Many mail clients, such as those built into Mozilla and Evolution, can also be used to read `usenet` news messages.

There are over 50,000 newsgroups, some of them attracting dozens of new messages each day.

If you are setting up an ISP you may want to build an NNTP server that carries every newsgroup. This is a major task, requiring clusters of very high performance computers.

Alternatively you may want to set up a server for a limited number of groups for use on a LAN.

There are two approaches to setting up a restricted server:

- Use a normal news server package such as `inn`, but only set it up with a limited number of groups.
- Use a 'lightweight' server, such as Leafnode.

Both of these types of server require some setting up. Inn comes with a file, `/usr/share/doc/inn-2.3.3/INSTALL` which details all the steps in the installation process. Normally `inn` connects to one or more other systems, known as news peers. It exchanges messages with its peers, which in turn exchange with their peers, until the news articles have propagated through the whole of `usenet`. Setting up `inn` is not difficult, provided you go carefully through all the steps. There are two types of setup – the one used on large systems where the peers know about the system you are setting up, and the one used on smaller systems

where the news comes from and goes to a server at your ISP and
other programs, such as nntpsend, are needed to connect to the
rest of usenet.

Leafnode is much simpler. It is not included in all distributions
but it can be downloaded from http://www.leafnode.
org/. It needs a little setting up – you can choose which server
it will take its feed from. Once it is set up it will let you connect
from your newsreader and ask for any newsgroup that is carried
on the server that feeds it. If that group is carried on Leafnode it
will let you see the articles in the group. If not it will make a note
that someone is trying to read that group, and fetch articles next
time it connects to the feeding server. In this way Leafnode is
completely automatic – users on your system can choose which
groups they wish to read and Leafnode will carry them.

7.4 Network security

7.4.1 Securing NNTP and SMTP

Having your own NNTP or SMTP server carries a potential
security risk. If your firewall or hosts.allow and
hosts.deny files are not set correctly anyone can connect from
the public internet and inject articles into usenet or e-mails into
the mail system, claiming that they are from your site.

The creatures which live under a damp stone at the bottom of
cyberspace, the pornographers and mail spammers, commonly
use *port scanners*, programs which hunt through blocks of IP
addresses for insecure NNTP and SMTP ports, then use these to
advertise their tawdry creations anonymously. It is a good idea
to test these ports from another machine elsewhere on the internet to make sure that they reject connections from the outside.
The test is very simple – from another site, with a different connection to the internet, use the telnet client program and try
to connect with the commands

```
telnet yourhost nntp
telnet yourhost smtp
```

in each case making sure that you get a 'connection refused'
message or no response at all.

You can perform a port scan on your own machine at the same
time with nmap. *Do not do this to someone else's machine un-
announced* – it looks like you are making an intrusion attempt.

Nmap and other security tools can be downloaded at
http://www.insecure.org/.

7.4.2 Introduction to firewalls

Inside the Linux kernel there is some code which does packet fil-
tering – it can look at incoming TCP/IP packets and decide to
accept them, drop them in the dustbin or send them home to the
originating computer with a note explaining why they have been
rejected.

The current version is known as iptables and replaces an
earlier packet-filtering system known as ipchains which was
not quite as versatile or easy to program.

Iptables works by keeping one or more tables of rules in
memory and using them to test message packets. Each table contains one or more chains – lists of rules in a particular order.

A rule is in two parts: the criteria and a target.

The kernel will test each packet against each rule in a chain to
see if it matches the criteria. If it does, the kernel will carry out
the action described in the target.

The iptables shell command adds, deletes and amends rules
and chains.

When you write a firewall you are in fact writing a series of commands to the iptables program, telling it how to set up the
rules in the way you want them.

There are two ways of writing a firewall. You can write a script
which issues commands to iptables directly. When you run
the script it will delete any old rules and create the new ones.
There is a good example of a Linux firewall written in this way
at http://www.linuxhelp.net.

Alternatively some distributions make use of the iptables-
save and iptables-restore commands. These convert a
complete firewall to a text file and back again. The text in the file
resembles very closely the commands to iptables.

Red Hat Inc.'s lokkit program creates a file called
/etc/sysconfig/iptables in this format, which is then
loaded as the firewall. You can create your own firewall by hand
and use it instead of this file.

The following is a simple firewall which I have written to illustrate how to create a suitable one for your machine.

```
# Manual firewall configuration. RB 8/5/03.

*filter
:INPUT DROP [0:0]
:FORWARD ACCEPT [0:0]
:OUTPUT ACCEPT [0:0]

# Refuse to forward anything originating on the internet
-A FORWARD -i ppp0 -m state --state NEW,INVALID -j DROP

# Pass anything originating in the LAN
-A INPUT -i eth0 -s 192.168.0.0/16 -j ACCEPT

# Similarly pass anything on loopback
-A INPUT -i lo -j ACCEPT

# The state machine rule that lets packets back in from
# the outside world
-A INPUT -m state --state RELATED,ESTABLISHED -j ACCEPT

# Accept the Unreachable, Time Exceeeded, Echo and Reply ICMPs
# This makes ping work.
-A INPUT -p icmp --icmp-type  3 -j ACCEPT
-A INPUT -p icmp --icmp-type 11 -j ACCEPT
-A INPUT -p icmp --icmp-type  8 -j ACCEPT
-A INPUT -p icmp --icmp-type  0 -j ACCEPT
-A INPUT -p icmp -j DROP

# Trap rejected connection attempts
-A INPUT -i ppp0 -m state --state NEW -j LOG --log-prefix REJ:
-A INPUT -i ppp0 -m state --state NEW -j DROP

COMMIT
*nat

# SNAT is similar to masquerade, replaces source
# address in outgoing
-A POSTROUTING -o ppp0 -j SNAT --to 158.152.132.30

COMMIT
```

The line '*filter' selects the table called 'filter' – the normal
default table – for the next few operations. The script then sets
up three chains, INPUT, FORWARD and OUTPUT. Packets
addressed to this machine go through INPUT, packets we generate go through OUTPUT, and FORWARD carries packets we receive
from one machine and pass on to another.

With a normal internet connection via an ISP you should only ever receive packets which are addressed directly to your computer. It is in theory possible to send you a packet addressed to another machine within your LAN. To do this would mean corrupting your ISP's routing tables, not an easy thing to do. Even if this happens the first rule will catch an intrusion attempt based on treating your firewall as a router.

The computer that uses this firewall is connected both to the internet and to a LAN. I trust the computers on the LAN – they are all mine – so I have a simple rule that accepts anything sent over the LAN interface. In the same way I trust myself, and accept any packet that comes from the same computer over the loopback interface.

The state machine rule accepts any packet that is a reply to one I have sent out. This lets me – for example – send a request for a web page to a server, and have the page itself allowed back through the firewall. If the server tried to send me a page un-invited it would simply crash into the firewall.

The next five rules let a selection of *internet control message protocol* packets through. These are needed to make `ping` and `traceroute` work. If you leave them out your computer will still work but it may have trouble with some network errors.

The next two rules have the same criteria and deal with forbidden connection attempts to this machine. The first rule makes a note in the system log of the rejected attempt. Because the `LOG` target does not terminate the scan, the next rule – which matches the same packets – destroys the offending connection attempts.

Together these two rules catch and slaughter malicious attempts to connect to a service within my machine from the internet proper.

The `COMMIT` line marks the end of rules for this table and triggers their transfer to the kernel.

The next few lines do the same thing for the `nat` table, which controls forwarding. In this case we take any packet that is going to go out on the `ppp0` interface and change its source address to be the same as the IP address of our connection to the internet.

A firewall will only stop intrusion attempts, it will prevent anyone outside the protected machine or LAN from connecting to anything inside. It can also be used to control outward connections:

you can create rules that will, for example, prevent certain machines on the LAN accessing particular websites.

The Censornet package http://www.censornet.com/ makes use of this to block offensive web content.

A firewall cannot filter out e-mail viruses. In the next section I will explain how viruses work and what can be done about them.

7.4.3 Viruses

A virus is a malicious program which is run by an unsuspecting user. It tries to replicate itself and damage the system it infects. Linux is inherently resistant to this kind of attack.

The virus problem exists because some packages (none of which run on Linux) see executable code in an arriving e-mail or imported word processor document, *and at once execute it.* On a system which does not have Linux's sharp distinction between ordinary users and root, a malicious program which is run as soon as a user opens an e-mail can do a lot of damage.

On Linux this does not happen. Incoming executable code is not executed unless the user chooses to run it. Even if the user does – we all make mistakes – the malicious program can only do what the user is allowed to do. If the user cannot damage the system neither can a virus.

7.4.4 Worms and exploits

A worm is a malicious program that replicates itself without human assistance. Worms are much rarer than viruses and relatively easy to kill.

A worm can only live at all if it can make use of a bug – usually in the mail transport software – which lets it do something it should not.

Making use of a bug in system software to get unauthorized access is called an exploit. Usually this means doing something outrageous and unexpected such as sending an e-mail with lines that are ten thousand characters long. This will cause some part of the system to fail in a way that can be manipulated by very subtle programming.

Killing a worm is simple – fix the bug that it uses, then examine every machine that it has touched to make sure it has made no malicious changes.

The major distribution manufacturers, in collaboration with the Common Vulnerabilities and Exposures Project at `http://cve.mitre.org/`, are progressively reviewing all vulnerable code in order to shake out bugs of this kind before they are exploited, with the result that they are now becoming extinct. All major distributions are backed up by regular security updates available over the net which fix bugs of this kind.

Checking a machine for damage is relatively simple. The verify option of the `rpm` program can perform a basic check. The `tripwire` package performs a better test, and also can detect attacks on the `rpm` system itself. You can also use `tar` to compare your system against a known good backup.

7.4.5 Intrusion

Unauthorised access to a computer over a network, through services such as NFS, `telnet` or `ftp`, is called intrusion. It is not always malicious but it can be very destructive. You can detect and prevent intrusion attempts with a few simple steps.

- Set up your firewall to reject any connection attempts other than those you expect. If you are not using a firewall make sure that `/etc/hosts.allow` and `/etc/hosts.deny` create a barricade around all of your ports, letting through only the very few accesses you choose to permit.
- Use `ssh` in preference to `rsh`, `telnet` and `rlogin`, disable the other protocols by editing files in `/etc/xinetd.d`.
- Periodically check `/var/log/messages` for rejected connections and authentication failures. Investigate any that you do not understand. Make yourself unpopular by demanding explanations.
- Make sure that your `/etc/exports` file is as restrictive as possible. Export filesystems read-only and with root squash if you can. Export only to IP addresses that have a legitimate reason for access. Exporting a scratch area is often safer than exporting all or part of `/home`.

7.4.6 Psychological pointers to security risks

You can often anticipate breaches of security by noticing one of these common situations – all of which I have seen.

- 'You're fired!' But he still has the root password.
  Make sure that you change all critical passwords at once.

- 'I wonder what happens if I try . . . Oh dear.'
  Anything important needs to be properly secured. Create a
  safe place for anyone who wants to try out ideas. Remember
  that employees' bright ideas can often save you money. The
  person who wants to experiment usually intends to develop
  skills which will become an asset to you.
- 'Where does he get the money from?' He's selling data to
  your competitors.
- 'It can't happen here.' It's probably happening now.

7.5 Network caching

If you have several users on one or more machines sharing a connection to the internet they will probably make a habit of visit-
ing the same pages regularly. They will all use expensive
bandwidth to download the same background images, then fill
up their disk caches with lots of identical files.

You can limit this problem by adding a *web proxy cache*, such as
Squid. This is included with many distributions or can be downloaded from http://www.squid-cache.org/. Squid takes
requests for web pages from users' browsers and forwards them
to the real web servers. It keeps a cache of recently visited pages
on disk. If it is asked for a page or image which is already in the
cache it will give its cached copy to the browser without request-
ing it from the remote server.

Squid is very simple to set up. Once the package has been
installed you can edit /etc/squid/squid.conf to set Squid's
options. Most of the default settings will do – you need only
check that the *Access Control List* (ACL) is correct for your
system. The file /usr/share/doc/squid-(version)
/QUICKSTART – substitute the version number of the copy of
Squid that you are running for (version) – tells you how to get
Squid running quickly.

It is very important that you make sure your cache is secure, in
the sense that it will not accept requests from outside your LAN.
If you set up a cache which is available to the outside world,
sooner or later someone else will find it and either use it to
save themselves time or, even worse, to distribute questionable
material.

Having set up and secured your cache you can now go to your
browser's preferences and for each protocol that you would like

to cache, normally HTTP, FTP and Gopher, set the address of the cache machine and the port on which the cache listens. This is normally port 3128. The Gopher protocol is becoming rare, having been largely superceded by the World Wide Web.

Once you have a working cache you can reduce the amount of disk cache used by individual users' browsers, possibly eliminating it altogether. This will save disk space and backup time.

If you want to use one computer as the cache for an entire LAN you must choose one that is fast enough to handle the network and disk traffic involved. This is not a good application for an old, slow machine.

Squid keeps log files in /var/log. You can look at these if you need to track down the cause of a problem with Squid – a rare event – or to identify the cause of the problem if the cache is being misused.

When you connect to a secure server that uses an encrypted protocol to carry sensitive data, for example when you use online banking, Squid cannot cache or even understand the traffic between browser and server. When a secure connection is established, the computer at each end sends a public key to the other. The public key is sufficient to encrypt a message for the computer that sent it out, but the corresponding private key, which is kept secret by the sender, is needed to decrypt it again. Creating the public key from the private one takes microseconds, reversing the operation would take many years of computation. Each computer receives the other one's public key and can send secret messages to the other but anyone listening to the connection cannot find out what the private keys are – and therefore cannot read the messages.

Squid simply *tunnels* secure connections – passes them through completely unmodified. In almost all cases this is exactly what you want to have happen.

08
maintaining the system

In this chapter you will learn:

- how to install, configure and remove software
- how and when to make backups
- how to recover from a disaster
- what to do about common problems

In this chapter I will explain some operations that you can do to add new features to your system, make it secure against hardware failures and put right a few things that can go wrong. A Linux system can almost always be repaired if things come badly adrift – a mercifully rare event in any case. Complete loss of data, except in the case that the hardware has self-destructed, is almost unknown.

Hardware failures, particularly disk-drive problems, happen all the time to computers regardless of the operating system they are running. One of the major advantages of Linux is that it enables you to deal with them quickly and easily.

Disk drives have become vastly more reliable in the thirty years since I first entered the computer industry, regardless of the fact that they depend on a near-impossibility to function at all. In Chapter 1 I mentioned briefly how a hard drive works – how the heads face the platters without quite touching them. In fact there is a minute air gap between head and platter. This gap is so small that the relationship of head, air gap and platter is, to scale, comparable with taking a fighter aircraft through the sound barrier at an altitude that would be considered minimal for a lawnmower.

This does not always work. The phenomenon known as a head crash, in which the head actually touches the platter with terminal results for both, is very rare but very sudden. When it happens the bulk of the data on the drive has gone to join the snows of last year.

Being aware of this, and planning for it, is one of the basic system management skills that you can learn with a Linux machine.

8.1 Installing, configuring and removing packages

Many Linux systems use the *Redhat Package Manager* (RPM), originally developed by Red Hat Inc. to install and maintain optional software.

RPM works with packages, which are archives with some additional control information. The archive part is in a format called cpio, and the program rpm2cpio can remove the control information leaving just the archive.

RPM keeps a database of the packages which are installed on your system, normally in /var/lib/rpm. For each package it holds a list of the files included in the package, their ownerships, permissions and checksums.

Using the database RPM can track down every file that should be part of a package, wherever it is on your system. It can check for files having been altered, so it can detect almost all accidental or malicious damage to the system.

RPM can delete all the files making up a package. In most cases this means that it works as a totally clean 'uninstall' – it can put a system back to exactly where it was before a package was installed.

RPM can also be used to create packages, a process I will describe in Chapter 12.

RPM can also install and create source rpm files which are compressed archives of the source and script files needed to create a package.

The everyday uses of RPM are these:

- Install a package. Type

  ```
  rpm -i package
  ```

  as root. The package parameter is the path – relative or absolute – to the file containing the package you want to install. It should end in .rpm.
- Upgrade a package. This command replaces an installed package with a later version. When the manufacturer of the distribution you are using releases an improved version of a package you can download the new .rpm file. Then type

  ```
  rpm -U package
  ```

  as root. Note that it is a capital U to avoid confusion with an obsolete -u option.
- Erase (uninstall) a package. This deletes all the files associated with the package. Type

  ```
  rpm -e name
  ```

  where name is the name of the package, not a file name.
- Verify a package. This command

  ```
  rpm -V name
  ```

  will check all the files associated with the database and report any problems.

When RPM installs a package it makes an entry in the database. That entry is named with the package name and version. You can use the command

```
rpm -qa
```

to find out the names of all the packages installed on your system. For example if one of these names is

```
gnome-utils-1.0.50-4
```

you can use the package name gnome-utils to refer to the installed package in the -e and -V commands.

Downloading and installing a package on your system lays it open to a particular type of threat – a package which has been in some way modified to compromise security. It is possible, with a certain amount of programming skill, to construct a package which looks like a legitimate upgrade but which in fact breaches your security. To prevent this the distribution manufacturers add public-key signatures to packages which can be checked before the package is installed. Use the command

```
rpm --checksig package
```

to test the validity of a signature.

Many distributions now have GUI interfaces to package managers. If you have downloaded a package, and can see it in a folder on your desktop, you may be able to install it simply by clicking on it. Alternatively you may find a tool to add or remove packages in the system menu.

8.2 Making backups

The purpose of making backups is to be sure that you can get your computer working again as quickly as possible if something catastrophic happens to it, and to ensure that you lose very little data.

Hard drives fail. When they fail they lose data. The path to safety lies through making lots of copies.

8.2.1 Backup tools

There are several tools you can use to make backups:

- Zip. This program converts part of a filesystem tree to a *zipfile*, normally with the file type .zip, which contains all the files in the tree in a compressed form. The major advantage to zip is that it is compatible across a large number of operating systems. It also understands text files, and can convert between the formats used on a range of systems. Its drawback is that it does not completely understand the Linux and UNIX filing systems, so a backup made with zip is not guaranteed to restore perfectly. In particular, it does not understand special files – you cannot use it to back up /dev. If you need to make backups which are readable on a machine running an operating system other than Linux, and you only need to make backups of ordinary files, use zip.

- Tar. The name is a contraction of 'Tape Archiver'. Tar can make perfect backups of Linux and UNIX systems. It converts a file tree of any complexity into a stream of bytes, and back again. It can call up programs to compress the stream if needed. Tar can operate magnetic tape drives directly – but it is not restricted to using tape as a backup medium. It can equally well backup to removable disks or, with a separate program to control the *burning* process, to recordable CDs. Tar archives can be read on almost any computer but can only be fully restored, including all the permissions, on another Linux or UNIX machine.

- Dump. This program, and its companion restore, have some useful features for making regular backups. Dump makes use of 'Dump Levels'. A dump at level 0 will include all the files in a system, at level 1 the files changed since the last level 0. Level 2 will take files changed since the last level 1 and so on to level 9.

Both dump and tar were originally intended for the big open-reel tape drives that were beloved of 1960s' film producers. A row of drives rewinding or searching provided an instant, if incomprehensible, leitmotif for the computer throughout an entire decade.

The tape drives of the period usually recorded data on seven or nine tracks with a density of about 800 bits per inch in each track. A 2400-foot reel of tape had a capacity of around 20 megabytes – a little more than a box of modern floppies. This was larger than many of the disk drives in use at the time.

The tape handling commands of both dump and tar still work in the same way, even though the capacity of the media they now use has increased a thousandfold.

Tar has the ability to pipe the archive through a compression or decompression program. This makes the archive smaller – typical compression ratios are around three to one – at the expense of slowing down the backup process. The compression programs available, and the options to select them are:

- -Z Compress uses Lempel–Ziv compression, named after the two mathematicians who developed it. It has largely been superceded by gzip.
- -z Gzip also uses Lempel–Ziv. In its other guise as gunzip – the corresponding decompression program – it is compatible with compress.
- -j Bzip2 uses Burrows–Wheeler compression which is slightly more effective than Lempel–Ziv.

Gzip – selected with the z option – is the most usual, followed by Bzip2.

An uncompressed tar archive normally has the file type .tar, one compressed with gzip .tgz or .tar.gz and where Bzip2 compression is used .tbz or .tar.bz2.

Both tar and dump can split their output into manageable sections, but neither does it in a way that is convenient for making backups to writable CD-ROMS and similar media. There are a number of third-party utilities available on http://www.linux.org to deal with this problem, and to manage backups in general. I have also written a program to do this for my own use, called tsplit. It is available under GPL. There is more about tsplit in Chapter 12.

Both KDE and GNOME know about tar archives. You can click on an archive file on the desktop and you will see the files it contains.

8.2.2 Regular backups

To make your data as safe as possible you should have a plan for your backups. Some parts of the system, which change infrequently, need only be backed up every week, or when you know you have made a change. The areas in which you are working need more frequent backups.

Once you have your system working to your satisfaction you can either add a backup program or write a few lines of script to make backups from the command line or by clicking on the desktop.

If you are working on something that is changing rapidly you may want to make very frequent backups. One way to do this is to run a `cron` job which copies the files you are changing to another disk drive. Note that it must be a different drive, not another area on the same one, so that if one drive fails the data on the other will probably survive. This script runs every 15 minutes from `cron` (I have had to split the line that begins 'tar' to make it fit on the page: that and the next one should be all one long line):

```
#!/bin/sh
# Regular backup of what I'm working on
tar -czf /seagoon/unclebob/$(date +%a%H%M).tgz
     $(find Desktop -ctime -1 -type f) axhome/backup
find /seagoon/unclebob/ -ctime +7 -exec rm {} \;
```

The section

```
$(find Desktop -ctime -1 -type f)
```

calls the find program to make a list of all files on the desktop or in folders on the desktop that have changed during the last day. These, and the files in `axhome/backup` which is where the word processor keeps a copy of the file I am working on, are backed up to `/seagoon/unclebob`, which is on a different drive. The last line finds and deletes backups which are more than a week old. By this time the changes will have found their way into my ordinary backups. You can see how this works by looking at the manual pages for find and date.

EXERCISE

8.1 The automated backup in this section fails for file names which contain spaces. Why? How can this be fixed?

8.2.3 Backing up dual-boot systems

If you have a dual-boot system, and the other operating system uses a filesystem that Linux cannot write, you can still back up that operating system using Linux.

To make this work well, prepare the hard disk before you install the operating systems. Bring up a version of Linux that does not need the hard drive – the rescue mode of your distribution will normally work like this – and use this command:

```
dd if=/dev/zero of=/dev/hda
```

o write zeroes over the whole of your hard drive before you
tart. *This will erase all the data on your hard drive.* If your hard
rive is not the first IDE disk – for example it might be /dev
sda if it is a SCSI drive – use its name in place of /dev/hda.

hen install your operating systems, adding Linux last. For
xample you might install Linux in /dev/hda5 and another
perating system in /dev/hda1.

Make a careful note of the partition table, you will need it if you
ave to restore the backup.

When Linux is running you can use a command like this

```
zip </dev/hda1 >othersys.gz
```

o back up the other system.

his treats the whole of the other system as one big file and com-
resses it into othersys.gz. Because you filled the disk with
eroes, the other system's free space – the areas of its partition
hat have never been used – will still contain nothing but zeroes,
nd the gzip compression program will reduce them to almost
othing.

his backup can be restored with the command

```
unzip <othersys.gz >/dev/hda1
```

hich simply reverses the process. This is not really a satisfactory
ay of making backups. These files can only be restored to a par-
tion with exactly the same geometry. There is no guarantee that
his sort of backup will restore at all to a drive with a different
umber of heads or sectors.

he real virtue of this is that it lets you use a Linux system to
ake a snapshot of another system, and restore it quickly. If you
re about to do something irreversible, such as installing an
pdate, this type of backup will let you recover gracefully if
omething goes badly wrong.

.2.4 Backup media

here are several kinds of backup media you can use.

Magnetic tapes. The drives are relatively expensive and this
technology is falling out of favour.
Removable disks. These are similar to hard disks, but the
disk platters are contained in a replaceable cartridge.

- Recordable CDs and DVDs. At the time of writing this is the preferred technology for volume backups. Both drives and media are relatively cheap. Almost all the drives available at the moment are fully supported by Linux.

Some of these drives can perform operations – such as erasing the media – for which there are no standard IDE commands, even though they are connected to your computer's IDE bus. The IDE-SCSI driver deals with this by making some IDE devices appear to be SCSI devices as well. Software which works with the SCSI version of a particular drive will usually work with the IDE device through this driver. To use this driver set a kernel parameter so that, as Linux starts up, the device will be 'claimed' by the IDE-SCSI driver. For example, if your IDE/ATAPI CD writer is /dev/hdc, setting the parameter

```
hdc=ide-scsi
```

will make it appear as /dev/scd0 instead – a SCSI device which can be used with the CD-writing software. This parameter has to be set in your LILO or GRUB configuration. I will explain how to do this in Chapter 9.

8.2.5 Specifics for Iomega drives

Iomega Corporation, which can be found at http://www.iomega.com, make a number of removable media products, many of which are compatible with Linux. The Iomega 'Zip Drive', which should not be confused with the program called zip, is manufactured in a variety of different forms. I have bought three of these drives over several years for different machines and found them to work well with Linux.

The Zip cartridge is a removable hard disk, with a capacity between 100 and 750 megabytes. As supplied, the cartridges have a partition table with primary partition four set up to be the whole disk. If your Zip drive is /dev/sda, for example, the partition /dev/sda4 will be the whole disk, and can be mounted in the usual way.

It is possible to repartition a Zip cartridge with the fdisk program – and even install Linux onto it.

Zip drives come with driver software for a variety of operating systems. There is also a program which can be downloaded from Iomega's website to operate the Zip drive's protection features from the Linux command line.

If a Zip cartridge is reformatted on an Apple Macintosh computer using the HFS filesystem it can still be mounted on a Linux machine. This is described in detail in Chapter 3.

If you use a Zip drive with some other operating systems, but without installing the drivers, the Zip drive may be treated as a large floppy. If this happens the partition table is erased and the entire disk is formatted with the other system's filing system. Linux can still read and write a cartridge in this state. You can mount it as `/dev/sda` instead of `/dev/sda4` and use it normally.

8.2.6 Using `tar`

There are two kinds of command line options to `tar`.

The first kind of options are functions. There are eight of these, and every command to `tar` must contain exactly one function option. The four you will need are:

- `-c`   Create an archive from one or more files.
- `-x`   Extract files from an archive.
- `-d`   Find differences between files and an archive.
- `-t`   List the files in an archive.

The other options modify what `tar` does. The ones you will use most often are:

- `-z`   Use `gzip` compression.
- `-j`   Use `Bzip2` compression.
- `-N date`   Only process files newer than the given date.
- `-f path`   The archive is in a file.
- `-l`   Stay in one filesystem.
- `-v`   Be verbose – list files as they are processed.

The date parameter to the `-N` option can be in a variety of formats. The easiest one to remember is

```
YYYY-MM-DD HH:MM:SS
```

note that the objects get smaller from years at the left to seconds at the right. This makes it a very easy format to remember. For example I am drafting this paragraph at

```
2003-03-31 15:23:31
```

which is just over twenty-three and a half minutes past three on Monday 31st March 2003. Because this date format has a space in the middle it must be wrapped up in quotes to tell `tar` that it is all one parameter, like this:

```
-N "2003-03-31 15:23:31"
```

The -1 (local) option tells `tar` to ignore any mount points it finds within the tree that it is backing up. You should use this if you want to make a backup of the root filesystem of a running system, otherwise `tar` will try to back up all the other mounted filesystems, including /proc which is potentially very large, and filesystems mounted over the network.

I have often found it useful either to have a CD-ROM with a standalone system on it handy for making backups or, if there is enough disk space available, to install Linux twice. The main installation contains everything I need to work normally. The second 'maintenance' installation is text-only and contains an absolute minimum of packages. It can be brought up to make a completely clean backup of the main system – nothing can change the main system's files while a backup is in progress.

When making backups it is a good idea to think about how you are going to restore the system from them. In particular, if you make backups onto CD-ROMs you need to have some way of bringing your system up from your CD drive, and *then using the same drive to restore your backups*. I will explain some ways of doing this in a later chapter.

If you are using CD-ROMs as your backup medium you can make a single disk that will restore your maintenance partition. Log in as root, then copy the first disk of your distribution, using the -a option to the `cp` command, to a new directory on your hard disk. Next remove the contents of the directory which contains the packages – `RedHat/RPMS/` on RedHat systems. Now make a backup of your maintenance partition with `tar` and place it in the new directory. You may also find it useful to put `fstab` and the partition list (see next section) into this directory.

Burn a bootable CD from this directory as described in Chapter 4. You can now use it to bring up the rescue system, and reinstate the whole machine.

8.2.7 Backup planning

It is useful to make a plan for backing up your data. Once you have installed Linux it is a good idea to make a *full backup* of your whole installation as soon as possible.

At the same time it is worth making a note of where your partitions are on disk and their mount points. The easiest way to list your partitions is with the command

```
fdisk -1 >partitionlist
```

Note that this may have a few side-effects as it tests every disk drive on your system. Avoid using this command when, for example, burning a CD or doing anything else that will not tolerate being held up for a few seconds. Save `partitionlist` and `/etc/fstab` along with your full backup in case you need to recreate the partition table later.

From then on you need only back up the files you are actually working on. You can do this either by hand – simply drag and drop them to backup disks, copy them with a shell command or manually run an archive program. `Tar`'s -N option – only back up files newer than a given date – is useful for this. Once you have a little experience with shell scripting you might like to make these *incremental backups* automatic.

For example you could have a script that makes a full backup, something like this:

```
tar -clzf /mnt/removable/fullbackup.tgz /
date "+%F %R:%S" >lastfull
```

This makes the backup then writes the time and date to 'lastfull'. You can later make a backup of files changed since that date with:

```
tar -N $(cat lastfull) -clzf /mnt/removable/inc.tgz /
```

The second script uses the contents of the file called `lastfull`, which was automatically written when the full backup was made, to supply the parameter to the -N option. Files with time-stamps later than this will be backed up.

Note that all of these scripts must be run as root so that they can back up every file on the system.

8.2.8 Offsite copies, checkpoints and media cycling

Backups are useful only if you can restore them. I have one particularly horrifying memory of a financial institution who, back in the 1970s, made three copies of their customer database, put them all on the same shelf, and closed down for Christmas. When they came back they found that a water pipe had burst above the shelf *destroying every copy*. Fortunately some scratch disks that had been used earlier contained the same data and were on the other side of the room.

When you make a plan for how you will organize your backups it is worth designing in some way of making offsite copies. These should ideally be full backups. If you are using the sort of script that is in the previous section do not let offsite copies change the saved last full backup date, otherwise your incremental backups may not contain everything they should.

Keep your offsite copies off site. For many years I have plagued my relatives and friends with requests to look after small boxes of disks. And just once I have been very glad that I did when an accident destroyed an onsite copy. Physical separation is what matters. If there are twenty miles between two copies of your data it is unlikely that any one accident can destroy both.

If you use media such as Zip disks for backups you may choose, because of the cost of the disks, to reuse them. This is normally a good plan. Have, say, three sets of disks and use them in rotation for daily backup, and another three for weekly. Figure 8.1 shows a typical sequence for this sort of backup scheme. In each case the oldest backup disk in a particular cycle is overwritten by the new information. The daily backup disks are overwritten twice per week, the weekly backups every three weeks.

However, if you make a mistake in editing a file, three weeks later the error has cycled into every backup disk and you have lost the original, unedited version. To avoid this, consider taking a check point copy at least as often as your slowest regular backup takes to cycle. This is not a perfect solution, but it very much improves your chances of being able to find a lost file again. The check-point copies should be kept 'for ever' which means in practice until you can get them copied onto cheaper media.

This is not a problem if you use one-time writable media for your backups. In this case you can simply keep everything, or at least a good sample.

The final danger associated with backups is known as *media cycling*. I have seen even experienced operators caught out by this. What happens is that a disk cartridge becomes damaged. This is then put in a drive which does not have a full headcrash but a minor bump between platters and head, sufficient to damage the head. The backup turns out to be unreadable. The temptation at this point is to put the next oldest backup in the drive and try again. Then the damaged head scores the surface of that disk and makes it unreadable. Panic now begins to set in and, in a frantic attempt to find *any* working media *every* cartridge in the room is tried and ruined. The problem is more acute where more than one drive is available – the worst case of this I have seen wrote off three drives and about a dozen cartridges.

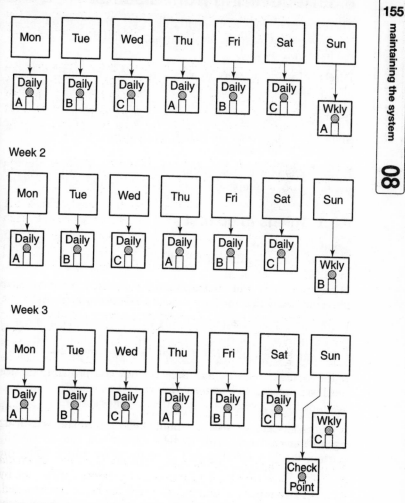

Figure 8.1 Typical backup sequence using six disks

The way to avoid this is to stop after one unexpected error, take stock of the situation and look for the cause of the problem. If you have to try a second cartridge in the suspect drive, use a scratch cartridge that does not contain vital data. If this does not work, *have an engineer look at the drive* before doing anything else.

8.3 Recovering from disasters

There are two kinds of computer disaster: those that are caused by software but leave the hardware intact, and those that destroy the hardware as well.

Purely software disasters are very rare with Linux machines and almost always traceable to a hardware problem, or to a serious blunder by someone logged in as root. After a software disaster it is always possible to restore everything from backups, and quite often to recover anything entered up to a few minutes before the catastrophe.

In this section I will walk through the sequence of actions you can use to restore a completely dead computer to normal operation.

8.3.1 Things to do first

Begin by trying to bring the machine up. If you can get as far as the boot loader – LILO or GRUB – and you have multiple boot installed, try each operating system in turn. Bringing up a system other than Linux will not help with the recovery, but it will give you confidence that the hardware is all working correctly.

If you can get any version of Linux to come up you can use it to repair the rest of the system. This is where the maintenance partition can be very useful as it usually survives most disasters.

If the system comes up and then crashes you probably do no need to restore from backups. The next section makes some suggestions for recovering a system that will not stay up.

If you cannot get the system to boot at all the next step is to bring up a rescue system. With RedHat Linux you can do this by putting the first installation CD in the drive and booting the machine, then typing

```
linux rescue
```

at the prompt. A Knoppix CD can also be used as a rescue system.

It is quite possible that the cause of the problem is that the boot loader has been corrupted, possibly by using an installation or disk partitioning program that has damaged the first block on the hard disk.

If this is the case you can restore the boot loader from the rescue system.

8.3.2 Restoring the GRUB boot loader

From the rescue system try to mount your root partition read-only. The RedHat rescue system will give you an option to do this automatically. If you cannot use this try mounting manually, type

```
mkdir /mnt/sysimage
mount /dev/hdax /mnt/sysimage
```

replacing `hdax` with the real identity of your root partition.

You can now run the GRUB program by typing

```
/mnt/sysimage/sbin/grub
```

The way GRUB describes disk drives and partitions is not the same as the method used by the running system. GRUB needs to find where the 'stage1' program is stored on your disk, and build this information into the initial loader that it installs at the beginning of your hard disk. There are three steps to this process.

1 Find the `stage1` program. If you know where it is you can skip this step. If not, you can use GRUB to find it. The program is in a file that will have the path `/boot/grub /stage1` on the running system. If you have a separate partition that will be mounted as `/boot` the file will be `/grub/stage1` within that partition. If you do not have a separate boot partition `/boot` will be a directory within your root partition and the path to the file will be `/boot/grub/stage1`.

To find the boot loader if you have a separate boot partition type

```
find /grub/stage1
```

if you have one big partition type

```
find /boot/grub/stage1
```

and if you do not know, try both.

When GRUB finds the loader it will display something like

```
(hd0,4)
```

which means 'Partition 4 on hard drive 0'. If you have more than one version of Linux installed choose the one you want to boot – the partition numbers displayed by GRUB may not be the same as the partitions displayed by `fdisk`, but they will be in the same order.

2   Tell GRUB which partition to use. Type this command

```
root (hdx,y)
```

replacing x and y with the values that the find command gave you.

3   Write the initial loader to disk. Type

```
setup (hd0)
```

to write the loader to the first block of the first hard disk. You can use a different drive name in place of hd0 to write the loader in another place, but hd0 will be correct for the vast majority of computers.

You can now leave GRUB with the quit command and type exit to reboot your computer.

8.3.3 Restoring the LILO boot loader

The LILO boot loader works in a different way. The installation process locates everything on the disk that LILO can load and builds its location into the loader.

Restoring LILO involves setting up the system so that the partitions it references are mounted in their correct relationship to one another.

For example, if you have a / (root) partition in /dev/hda7 and a /boot partition in /dev/hda5, they will not be mounted on those mount points by the rescue system. If you let the rescue system mount them as /mnt/sysimage and /mnt/sysimage/boot – or do the same thing manually – you can reinstall LILO by typing this command:

```
/mnt/sysimage/sbin/lilo -r /mnt/sysimage
```

How this works is that the -r option tells LILO to change root to /mnt/sysimage. LILO sees /mnt/sysimage as the root filesystem – to LILO this is /. As far as LILO is concerned /mnt/sysimage/boot is /boot. LILO then reads its configuration file, which refers to files in the /boot directory, finds them in the right places and reinstalls itself.

The same principle applies to any other filesystems that are mentioned in /etc/lilo.conf. Provided they are mounted in the right places relative to the root filesystem, LILO will find them and install their boot options.

8.3.4 Is this partition recoverable?

It is very rare for an `ext2` or `ext3` filesystem, even under extreme provocation, to disintegrate to the point that no data can be recovered. Turning off power to the computer during a write operation normally leaves `ext2` in a recoverable state, and has almost no effect on `ext3`. Massive corruption of RAM, such as happens when a memory module falls out of its socket, can cause random data to be written to a drive, but even this is rarely terminal.

If a partition appears to be corrupt, the first thing to do is to try to mount it read-only, before you make any attempt to repair it. You can do this in the rescue system with a command such as

```
mount /dev/hdax /mnt/sysimage -o ro
```

once again replacing the `x` with the appropriate partition number.

If you can mount a corrupt partition this way you should regard the data on it as having had a stay of execution, not a reprieve, and at once copy anything changed since the last backup to a safe place.

The next step is to unmount the affected partition and use the `fsck` command to check it. Once again in the rescue system type

```
fsck -f /dev/hdax
```

The `-f` option forces `fsck` to perform a check, even if the partition is flagged as not needing one.

This will probably report errors, and ask you for your permission to correct them. You can either accept or reject each change `fsck` offers, or simply restart it with the `-p` option as well as the `-f` to accept all the suggestions. This will nearly always put the filesystem back together again. Even if it fails it may find some of the lost files and move them to the `lost+found` directory. Unfortunately it does not recover the file names, you may have to use `grep` to search the `lost+found` directory for a missing file.

8.3.5 Using the `fdisk` program

The `fdisk` program which you can use to repartition a disk accepts a few very simple commands.

Fdisk is a very powerful tool and using it carelessly can destroy information on a hard disk. Only use `fdisk` when you know that you need to examine or edit a partition table.

To examine the partition table, type

```
fdisk -l /dev/hda
```

or you can use /dev/hdb for the second IDE disk, /dev/sda for the first SCSI or USB disk and so on. It is a good idea to do this and either print the results or copy them down from the screen before you do anything else, in case you want to reverse your changes later.

To edit the partition table, enter

```
fdisk /dev/hda
```

with no options. You can edit the partition table of a disk which has mounted filesystems, but it is an unsafe thing to do. To edit the partition table of the hard disk that your operating system boots from, use the rescue system. Only use fdisk from a running system if you are partitioning a disk which has nothing mounted.

Fdisk will display a prompt. To make sure everything is working enter the p (print table) command. You will see something like this:

```
Command (m for help): p

Disk /dev/hda: 255 heads, 63 sectors, 2432 cylinders
Units = cylinders of 16065 * 512 bytes

   Device Boot  Start   End   Blocks    Id System
/dev/hda1  *       1   616  4947988+    7 HPFS/NTFS
/dev/hda2         617  2432 14587020    5 Extended
/dev/hda5         617   629   104391   83 Linux
/dev/hda6         630   756  1020096   82 Linux swap
/dev/hda7         757  2425 13406211   83 Linux
/dev/hda8        2426  2431    48163+   6 FAT16
```

From then on you can use the n command to make new partitions, the d command to delete them and the t command to set the type of a partition.

The partition types are used by both Linux and some other operating systems to decide what sort of data is to be put into a partition.

The first four partitions on a hard drive are known as 'primary' partitions and some operating systems – not Linux – treat them specially. The example above is from a machine which is set up for dual boot: Microsoft Windows 2000 in partition 1 and the Linux boot partition in 5.

One of the first four partitions can be designated as 'Extended' – fdisk will give you an option to create this sort of partition when you enter the n command. You can then create 'Logical' partitions with numbers of 5 and above inside the extended partition. The cylinder numbers in the example illustrate this. Primary partition 1 runs from cylinder 1 to 616, extended partition 2 is from cylinder 617 to cylinder 2431. The logical partitions, 5 to 8, now fit end-to-end inside the extended partition.

You can always use the q command, or press **Ctrl-C**, to break out of fdisk. This is a safe thing to do as fdisk will not change anything until you tell it to.

When you have finished editing your partitions look at them with the p command – you can do this at any time to check what you are doing – and if everything is correct you can now make your changes permanent.

Enter the w command to write the new partition table to disk. Fdisk will now try to make the kernel see the changes to the table. If there is a problem here you should reboot the machine at this point. To reboot either exit from the rescue system or press **Ctrl-Alt-Del**.

Any partition that contained a filesystem before you ran fdisk, and is in *exactly* the same place – same starting and ending cylinders – should be undamaged by repartitioning. Any partition that has changed in any way should be reformatted with mkfs or mkswap.

Fdisk does nothing to the contents of a partition. Moving it or changing its size with fdisk will not move the data or change the size of the filesystem.

8.3.6 The 'Dropping you into a shell' message

If a partition is corrupt you may see a message when you try to bring up the system which looks like this:

```
*** An error occurred during the file system check.
*** Dropping you to a shell; the system will reboot
*** when you leave the shell.
```

This is one of the very few cases in which a Linux machine will need human intervention to help it come up. You can now type the root password – or press **Ctrl-D** to try to go on with the startup.

If you type the root password the system will effectively log you in as root. You can now do anything you could do if the system had come up and you had logged in as root, or that you could have done with the recovery system.

In this shell you can use fsck to repair damaged filesystems, make backups or restore them, or simply erase a damaged partition with mkfs. You can also edit /etc/fstab to comment out the problem filesystem by putting a hash (#) character at the beginning of the line.

8.3.7 The 'You don't exist' message

This message is very rare unless you are using NIS. If the /etc/passwd file, which contains a list of users, is corrupt or missing the message, 'You don't exist. Go away' may be displayed. If you know why this has happened you may be able to restore /etc/passwd from a backup.

If this message comes out without explanation you should suspect that the system is seriously damaged, perhaps from a malicious intrusion attempt. Copy all recently changed data and consider rebuilding the whole system from a backup.

On systems using NIS this message may simply point to a problem with the NIS server, or the way you have NIS set up on the local machine.

8.3.8 Restoring a backup

If you really have lost the contents of a partition you may need to restore it from a backup. Figure 8.2 is a roadmap of the routes you can take.

If you are restoring a partition other than root – for example if you have /home in a different partition, or on a different drive, you may not be able to bring the system up fully until the missing partition is restored. You can get around this by bringing the system up in runlevel 1 – see the next chapter for how to do this. You may get the 'Dropping you into a shell' message, in which case you can give the root password and use the shell, or the system may come up, depending on the state of the partitions. Either way you will be able to get into a root shell. Once you have the root shell you can use these commands:

- fdisk – This command partitions a hard disk. If you are replacing a hard disk or adding a new one you can use it to set up the partition table.

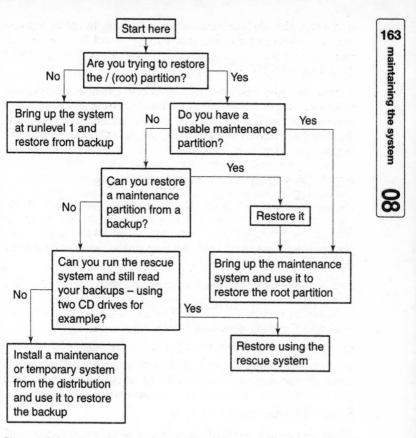

Figure 8.2 Possible routes to restoring a backup

- mkfs – Mkfs creates an empty filesystem inside a partition. By default it creates an ext2 filesystem but you can change this with the -t option. Once you have created a filesystem on a partition that partition can be mounted and used. Because mkfs creates an empty filesystem without reference to what is already on the disk it can also be used to erase everything from a corrupted partition before reusing it.
- tune2fs – You can use this command to adjust various parameters of a filesystem. The -j option will add a journal, converting an ext2 filesystem into ext3.
- tar – Use this to restore backups which are in .tar or .tgz format.

Be careful to check where the restored files are actually going. If you made a backup of a filesystem that was mounted as /home make sure that the appropriate partition is mounted as home in your current directory.

When tar makes an archive it removes the leading slash, if there is one, from the paths of files in the archive. So if you back up /home which contains /home/bob, /home/kathy and /home/stan they will appear as home/bob, home/kathy and home/stan in the archive. If you log in as root, and your working directory (you can check this with the pwd command) is /root, restoring a backup of /home will create the files in /root/home not /home. Tar is in fact doing the right thing here – removing the initial slash allows any backup to be restored anywhere. To restore this backup in the right place you should change your working directory to / with this command

```
cd /
```

then put the whole path to the backup on the command line, like this

```
tar -xzf /mnt/cdrom/backupofhome.tgz
```

or use the -C option to make tar run in a different directory

```
tar -C / -xzf /mnt/cdrom/backupofhome.tgz
```

in which case you do not need to change directories first.

Restoring the contents of a disk partition does not restore its label. If your distribution makes use of labelled partitions – look in /etc/fstab – you may need to use a command like this

```
tune2fs /dev/hda2 -L /
```

which changes the label of /dev/hda2 to /.

If you have made a backup of a maintenance partition on a bootable CD you can bring your computer up from the CD, type 'linux rescue' at the first prompt, then partition with fdisk, make a filesystem in the maintenance partition, mount it, restore the backup from the same CD and restore the boot loader.

When the system is operating normally the maintenance partition will be started by the main system's loader – LILO or GRUB. The loader for the maintenance system will be installed at the beginning of its partition. In order to start the maintenance system for the first time after a restore you may need to install its boot loader at the start of the hard disk, or keep an emergency boot floppy for the maintenance system handy.

Once you have the maintenance partition restored you can use it to put all the rest of your backups back onto the hard disk. You may then need to restore the boot loader a second time in order to make your main system, not the maintenance system, boot when your computer is started.

You can restore backups using just the rescue system if you have a way of making both the first distribution CD – with the rescue system – and the backup available at the same time. You can do this by installing two CD-ROM drives on one machine, or accessing a drive on another machine over the network.

If none of this works you can always go back to the distribution and install again, then restore /home from your backups to recover everything you were working on. Alternatively you can repartition your hard disk at this point and add a text-only maintenance system, then use it to restore all your other backups. If you do this you may need to edit /etc/fstab in the system you restore to match the new partitioning scheme.

8.3.9 Potential difficulties with restored files

Make a full backup of a filesystem, delete some files, move some others to a different directory, and then make an incremental backup. Now restore the filesystem from the full backup. Restore the incremental backup over it. All the deleted files will reappear, and the moved files will be in both places.

This is not really a problem – all that happens is that extra files turn up after a full restore and have to be deleted by hand. It is a potential problem when restoring to a partition that is nearly full. It may be necessary to stop after restoring the full backup and delete a few files that are known not to be wanted.

Some databases make use of 'sparse files'. These are files in which the individual data records are separated by large blocks of zeroes, which potentially can be filled in with information as the database is used. Linux can be set up to store these files efficiently by not allocating disk space to the unused areas. There are options you can set so that you can back up and restore this sort of filesystem without the unused areas becoming allocated during the restore. Look in the documentation for the database, and the manual page for tar.

Each file on an ext2 or ext3 filesystem has three timestamps. The 'last modified' time or mtime is a record of the time when the data in the file was last changed. The 'last changed' time or ctime records when the information held about the file in the directory entry, such as the permissions, was last altered. The 'last accessed' time or atime is a note of when the file was last accessed, even if it was only read.

The mtime is the timestamp that is normally displayed by the -l option to ls. You can see the atime with the options -lu and the ctime with -lc.

Reading a file changes the atime only. Writing to it changes the mtime as well. Changing its permissions with chmod changes the ctime but not the mtime or the atime.

When a file is backed up and restored with tar the mtime is kept but the atime and ctime are set to the time of the restore. The -N (--newer) option looks at *both* the mtime and the ctime and accepts the file for backup if *either* is later than the specified time.

If you restore your system from a full backup all the ctimes on all the files will change to the time of the restore. This will be later than the time of your last full backup. An incremental backup made with the -N option will now find that *every file in the system* is later than the specified time, and the incremental backup will become a full backup.

At the time of writing there is no convenient fix for this problem. Linux complies broadly with the POSIX standard, which defines what a running program can and cannot do. Unfortunately, it puts restoring the ctime from a backup in the 'cannot' category.

There are two ways around this problem. You can use the

```
--newer-mtime="YYYY-MM-DD HH:MM:SS"
```

form of the option, which ignores the ctime for your incremental backups. This will work, but occasional changes will not be backed up. The lost changes will not lose you any data if you have to restore again, but you may have to change the permissions on some files after the restore. Alternatively you can make a new full backup.

Do not try changing the saved time of the last full backup as a way of working around this problem unless you are keeping *every* backup for ever as you may find that some genuinely changed files are dropped from the backup as a result.

8.3.10 Replacing a hard disk

After you fit a new hard disk to a computer you can set it up for use like this:

1 Partition the disk with the `fdisk` command.
2 Make filesystems in the partitions with `mkfs`.
3 Adjust filesystem settings with `tune2fs` if required.
4 Copy or restore data into the partitions.

You can, as root, copy the whole of one filesystem to another with this command

```
cp -a /old/system /new/system
```

substituting the paths to your filesystems for `/old/system` and `/new/system`. As with `tar` this does not preserve the last changed time (`ctime`).

8.4 Common problems

This section is a collection of the system management problems that I have come across in the past few years, together with their solutions. If you have a system that will boot but will not then stay up you may find the solution here.

8.4.1 No space on hard drive

This can manifest itself in a number of ways. You may see a message saying 'No space on device' or something similar. It is also possible that one of the more space-hungry parts of the system, such as the GUI, may stop working.

Use the `df` command to see if any partitions have become full. If so you can use

```
du -sh /path/*
```

where `/path/` can be the path to any directory. This command will tell you how much disk space every subdirectory of `/path/` uses. Start at `/` and work downwards – usually the problem will be in either `/home` or `/tmp`.

A common culprit when all of your disk space has been stolen is a browser cache. Some web browsers can pull a frightening amount of data into their cache, only giving up when they run out of room on the disk.

8.4.2 Problems with /tmp directory

The `/tmp` directory is intended for storing temporary files which are discarded when the program using them exits. Many distributions have scavenging processes which will delete any file in /tmp which is more than a few weeks old.

Provided you stop the background processes – switch to runlevel 1 as described in Chapter 9 – you can, as root, safely delete every file in /tmp with the commands

```
cd /tmp
\rm -r *
```

note the backslash (\) character before the rm which overrides the confirmation prompts – rm will delete every file without asking you if it is doing the right thing. Be careful to type this command exactly as shown. *Check* that you are in the /tmp directory before you type \rm.

The /tmp directory must be writable by every user. If it is not, some programs, notably the X-Windows font server, can fail.

To check this use the command

```
ls -ld /tmp
```

The output from that command should look like this (ignore the date):

```
drwxrwxrwt 19 root root 4096 Apr 4 14:38 /tmp/
```

You can set the permissions – the usual cause of problems in this area – with the chmod command.

8.4.3 Hardware problems

Linux itself is extremely reliable. Most failures are traceable to hardware faults. When a hardware device is close to death it is quite common for the driver to detect a large number of errors before a failure occurs. The driver which is having problems sends error messages to your system log. The file /etc/syslog.conf – there is a man page explaining its format – controls where these messages go.

8.4.4 Problems with NFS servers

Once an NFS server is up and running it usually has no further problems. Difficulties with NFS are usually due to one of the following:

- Trying to start the server with a missing or empty /etc/exports file. If this happens you may see the message which indicates that the server has never started. Because NFS uses the RPC protocol it has to 'register' itself with RPC before it can receive requests from the outside world.

- Clock skew. Files created over NFS are given timestamps created from the clock on the server. These timestamps are then given out to client computers when the files are read. If the clock on the client machine is slow a file can appear to have a timestamp in the future. This can cause problems if you do anything that is sensitive to the order in which files were created, such as using the make program. The solution is to synchronize the clocks in all your computers. You can use the rdate command, run every few hours from cron, to do this.

- Address resolution. The NFS server will normally refuse connections if it cannot look up the client's IP address in either the /etc/hosts file or by using the DNS. Use the host, dig or nslookup commands to check your DNS if you have one. Log into the server and try to ping the client.

09

inside linux

In this chapter you will learn:

- how Linux starts up and shuts down
- what **init** scripts are and how you can use them
- what kernel modules are and how you can use them

This chapter is an introduction to some of the internal mechanisms of the kernel, and the programs and scripts that work closely with it. It is far from complete – a full explanation of the kernel alone would require a book several times the size of this one – but it covers the areas you are most likely to need.

9.1 The startup and shutdown sequences

This section explains how Linux starts up and shuts down, and how you can arrange to have extra things of your own – such as background programs – activated when your computer starts up.

9.1.1 How the kernel starts up

There are several loader programs that can be used to start Linux. LILO and GRUB are normally used with hard disks. Syslinux can load Linux from an MS-DOS format disk and is commonly used with floppies.

All the loader programs do the same thing. They read the contents of two files, the kernel and the initial *ramdisk*, into memory and start the kernel. These two files can be seen in the /boot directory. They have the names vmlinuz and initrd, followed by a version number. On this computer they are vmlinuz-2.4.18-27.8.0 and initrd-2.4.18-27.8.0.img.

The vmlinuz file is a compressed version of the kernel – the uncompressed version is vmlinux. There are major advantages to compressing the kernel – both in time and space – as it has to be loaded into memory by the BIOS, and often read from a floppy.

Once the kernel is in memory the loader program starts it. It then decompresses itself using a built-in program.

The loader can pass a command line to the kernel. You can use this line to set up kernel parameters which tell the kernel about non-standard hardware, set the runlevel or let the kernel know where its root filesystem is.

With LILO or syslinux you can type the parameters after the name of the system to be loaded, like this:

```
linux 3
```

to give the parameter 3 to the kernel. You can enter multiple parameters like this:

```
linux 3 lp=reset
```

which will also reset the printer port during startup.

The SuSE loader has a separate window for entering kernel parameters.

If you are using the GRUB loader you can edit the kernel parameters by typing 'a' when the GRUB screen appears. GRUB refers to the kernel parameters as 'kernel arguments'.

You can also make a permanent change to the kernel parameters by editing either /etc/lilo.conf or /boot/grub/grub.conf.

The kernel then finds the compressed initial ramdisk in memory, decompresses it and mounts it as the root filesystem.

Inside the initial ramdisk there is a file called linuxrc. The kernel runs this as a script. This script loads any modules you need – from the ramdisk itself – mounts the real root filesystem and then exits. Because of this mechanism the root filesystem can be on a disk which is accessed through a driver which is loaded as a module.

The kernel then tries to load and start the first task. It tries, in order, to run these programs /sbin/init, /etc/init, /bin/init and /bin/sh, and stops as soon as it finds one that works.

In effect this means it looks in three places for an init program, then if it cannot find one runs a shell.

The rest of the startup sequence is now controlled by the init program.

9.1.2 The init program

Init is the parent process of all other tasks and always runs with a *Process Identification* (PID) of 1.

The file /etc/inittab tells init how to set up the system. It first runs the system initialization script, normally /etc/rc.d /rc.sysinit, which manages most of the system startup. This script checks and mounts filesystems, loads modular drivers, sets up the time-of-day clock and performs a lot of similar operations.

When the sysinit script finishes, init chooses a *runlevel* for the system. This is a number in the range 0 to 6 which controls the type of system that will be started.

The assignment of meanings to runlevels varies between distributions. RedHat and SuSE both use these values:

1. Single-user system, suitable for troubleshooting.
2. Text-only system without NFS.
3. Text-only full system.
5. GUI-based system.

Debian uses runlevel 1 as the single-user system and 2–5 as multi-user.

You can set the initial runlevel in two ways:

- Edit the /etc/inittab file. The line

  `id:5:initdefault:`

  sets runlevel 5. You can change the 5 to any other suitable value.
- Tell the boot loader to tell the kernel as part of the kernel parameters. Put the runlevel you want in the kernel parameters as a single digit. Remember to separate the parameters with spaces.

Init will then enter the selected runlevel.

What happens next is controlled by the System V (often shortened to SysV) init scripts.

9.1.3 SysV init scripts

These are script files in the /etc/rc.d/init.d/ directory. They start and stop *services*, things your computer leaves running quietly out of sight, such as the daemon that works the printer. One script exists for every service that can run in background. These scripts can be run with a parameter which is one of the following:

- start   Start the background.
- stop   Stop the background.
- status   Show the status of the background.
- restart   Stop and restart the background.
- reload   Tell the background to reload its parameters.

You can run these scripts directly, indirectly with the command

`server service command`

or from GNOME by selecting

> System settings → Server settings → Services

and entering the root password.

When `init` enters a runlevel it runs the script `/etc/rc.d/rc`. This looks in one of the directories `/etc/rc0.d` to `/etc/rc6.d`, depending on the runlevel. These directories contain symbolic links to the scripts in `/etc/rc.d/init.d`.

These are a few typical links:

```
K74ntpd -> ../init.d/ntpd
K95firstboot -> ../init.d/firstboot
S05kudzu -> ../init.d/kudzu
S08iptables -> ../init.d/iptables
S09isdn -> ../init.d/isdn
S10network -> ../init.d/network
```

The link `K74ntpd` is a 'kill' link. When `init`, via the `rc` script, finds this link it will run the script that the link points to, in this case `ntpd`. Because this is a 'kill' link, beginning with `K`, the parameter given to the script will be 'stop'. Similarly the link `S09isdn` is a 'start' link and will run the `isdn` script with the parameter 'start'.

This mechanism is a little involved, but its practical purpose is very simple. Every `K` link in a particular runlevel kills off a service, every `S` link starts one. Because the links are numbered with the two digits between the `S` or `K` and the service name they are automatically sorted into order when the directory is listed, and as a result they are executed in numeric order.

By setting up just the symbolic links – and nothing else – you can control which services are started and stopped, and in which order, when the system enters a particular runlevel. Use the `chkconfig` command to manipulate the symbolic links.

The script `/etc/rc.d/rc.local` is run from a 'start' link in runlevels 2, 3, 4 and 5. You can edit this script to start private backgrounds, or to make final adjustments to hardware settings as the system comes up. This link is numbered 99, and so always runs last. This script, on one of my computers, starts a background that sends faxes, plays a sound clip to tell me that the computer is ready for work, and looks for life on other planets by starting a very low priority background task that processes SETI data, see `http://setiathome.ssl.berkeley.edu/`, (SETI being the Search for Extraterrestrial Intelligence).

If your computer has any older, non-standard serial ports you may need to set the port addresses and irqs for these devices. You can do this by putting commands in the file /etc/rc.serial (/etc/rc.d/rc.serial on some distributions) which is executed before init starts the services. This is an example of an rc.serial file from an older machine:

```
# RB 22 may 97, set correct IRQ for Rockwell modem
setserial /dev/modem irq 5
```

Note that in this case /dev/modem is a symbolic link to /dev/ttyS2. If you set up non-standard serial ports in this way you can start services, such as networking, which use them from the SysV init scripts.

9.1.4 The shutdown sequence

When you select the option to halt the computer, or use the shutdown command, you trigger a change to runlevel 0. Selecting reboot similarly changes to runlevel 6.

There are 'kill' links for all services in both /etc/rc.d/rc0.d and /etc/rc.d/rc6.d. Before your computer halts or reboots these shut down every service.

Both these runlevels call the script /etc/rc.d/halt. This script unmounts all the mounted filesystems, kills off all other tasks and sets the hardware clock to the time of day.

If the script /sbin/halt.local exists, the halt script will execute it as its last act before turning off or resetting the computer.

9.1.5 Starting and stopping NFS

If you are running an NFS server on your computer to share your files with other machines, the SysV init scripts will correctly take care of starting the network before the server, and stopping the server before network. Note that networking and the NFS server are both services and can be started and stopped from the command line or the 'Services' menu option in the GUI.

The system will normally try to mount all filesystems before it enters the initial runlevel. It cannot mount NFS filesystems, which are imported from other computers, until the networking service is started – which only happens when the SysV init scripts are run to enter that runlevel.

Nor can it dismount them with the local filesystems because networking is shut down when your computer enters a shutdown or reboot runlevel.

To get around this, Linux pretends that there is a service called netfs. This is started and stopped by the SysV init scripts in the usual way. It is not really a service – there is no background program associated with it – but starting it mounts all the NFS filesystems and stopping it unmounts them.

The NFS protocol is designed to cope with major interruptions to the network. It does this by holding up the tasks on the client machine that use files on the server until the problem has been cleared. This is normally what you want to happen. If you are copying a lot of files from one machine to another, and someone turns off the power to a hub somewhere between the machines, you want to be able to turn the hub on again and have the file transfer resume as if there had never been a problem. But if you are trying to shut down a machine which has a filesystem mounted on a server which cannot be reached – either because of a networking problem, or because the server itself has failed – the machine you are trying to shut down will wait for ever for the server to acknowledge the unmount request.

This problem has been inherited from older UNIX systems. NFS was originally intended for use with diskless workstations. Having no local disks, these workstations could safely be switched off without going through a proper shutdown sequence.

There are several things you can do about this:

- Use automount with NFS filesystems. This can reduce the probability that they will be mounted when the server fails.
- If you know that a server has failed, log in as root and unmount any filesystems mounted on it by hand. Using the -f option forces the dismount even if the server does not respond. This takes some time as Linux will wait for a response from the server, then do the dismount. You may need to use the fuser command to find out which tasks are still using the failed server and kill them first.
- Leave the machine as it is until the server is restarted.

Resetting the machine with the power switch is a last resort. If you are going to do this it is a good idea to wait until the machine has done nothing for thirty seconds. This gives Linux a chance to write information in memory back to disk, and improves the chances that the machine will restart cleanly.

A computer which has no disks, but mounts its root filesystem over the network, has to be able to access NFS before the network is started properly by the SysV init scripts. It does this by starting one network interface as part of the boot process. This is explained in Chapter 12.

9.1.6 Power failure

Linux uses a form of 'lazy write' with its disks. When a task wants to write to a file on disk Linux can put the information to be written on one side in RAM and deal first with another task's request to read a different file. The task that is writing does not care if its information is written to disk immediately, or a few seconds later. The task that is reading is held up – it cannot do anything until it has the information it needs. Linux will come back to the write request later and complete it.

If the power to the computer fails between the write request and the write operation actually happening you can lose data. In the few cases where this really matters you can use the sync command to force Linux to complete all pending write operations at once.

When you issue the sync command – it needs no options – it schedules all outstanding writes, but the command may complete while the writes are in progress. Using this command too often can slow down the whole system.

When your computer comes up Linux will check every ext2 or ext3 filesystem to see if it was properly unmounted last time it was used. If not – and this usually means that the power failed or someone pushed the reset button – Linux will try to restore the affected filesystem to an error-free, usable state. For ext2 filesystems it runs the fsck program which performs extensive consistency checks on the filesystem. With a large disk this can take many minutes.

Ext3 uses a 'journal', an invisible file in which it makes a note of anything that it is doing which could leave the filesystem in an inconsistent state. Linux recovers an ext3 filesystem by glancing at the journal and tidying up the affected parts of the disk.

EXERCISE

9.1 *WARNING. This exercise requires an external disk drive connected by a 'hot-swappable' bus, such as USB or FireWire.*

DO NOT attempt this with an internal drive, or one connected by SCSI or IDE – serious loss of data can result.

You will need an external disk drive such as a USB-connected Iomega Zip 100, and one cartridge which can be erased, for this exercise. Alternatively you can use a hard disk which can be connected over a hot-swappable bus or a 'keyring' flash device which plugs in to a USB port. *All the data on the disk you use will be erased.*

Connect the external disk drive and create one primary partition on it with `fdisk`. This should be partition number four. Make the partition type 83 (Linux).

Assuming that your disk is `/dev/sda` – substitute its real name if different – create an `ext2` filesystem on it with this command:

```
mkfs /dev/sda4
```

and create a mount point for it if you do not already have one with this command:

```
mkdir /mnt/zip
```

Now mount the disk with the command:

```
mount /dev/sda4 /mnt/zip
```

The next step is to cause a catastrophic dismount – the sort of thing that would happen if the power failed. *Very carefully unplug the USB or FireWire cable.*

If you now unmount the disk with the command

```
umount /mnt/zip
```

you will cause an error. It will be written to the log, and come up on the console if you have enabled system logging by editing `/etc/syslog.conf`. The error will look like this:

```
titania kernel: Device 08:14 not ready.
titania kernel: I/O error: dev 08:14, sector 10
```

You can safely ignore it. Now plug the cable in again and try to mount the disk again. You will succeed but this error – or something similar – will be reported.

```
EXT2-fs warning: mounting unchecked fs,
running e2fsck is recommended
```

Now unmount the disk and type this command:

```
fsck /dev/sdb4
```

The `fsck` program will recover the filesystem on the disk and show you what it is doing at each step. Enter the same command again and note that this time `fsck` finds nothing to do.

The command

```
tune2fs -j /dev/sda4
```

will add a journal to the filesystem, converting `ext2` to `ext3`. Mount it again now using the same command:

```
mount /dev/sda4 /mnt/zip
```

and once again unplug the cable and unmount the drive.

Now plug the drive in again and mount the drive – same command again. This time the `ext3` recovery will take over and you will see something like this in the log:

```
EXT3 FS 2.4-0.9.18, 14 May 2002 on sd(8,20),
            internal journal
EXT3-fs: recovery complete.

EXT3-fs: mounted filesystem with ordered data mode.
```

Compare the time taken by `fsck` to recover an `ext2` disk with the time taken for an `ext3` disk to recover itself from the journal.

9.2 Modules and drivers

The Linux kernel can be added to once it is running by loading kernel modules. These modules extend what the kernel can do. You can load a module to operate a digital camera, for example, or one that adds a networking protocol.

The advantage of using modules for these enhancements is that they can be loaded and unloaded while the system is running. Only the modules which are needed are loaded at any time, and they can be unloaded when they are no longer in use.

Because modules become part of the kernel they can do anything – change any data and access all the hardware. To prevent this becoming a security problem Linux imposes a restriction that only someone logged on as root can explicitly load and unload modules.

Any user can run this command

```
/sbin/lsmod
```

to see a list of the loaded modules. You can see the same information by looking at the /proc filesystem with the command

```
cat /proc/modules
```

which also works for any user.

When you load a module you can give it module parameters. These are instructions to the module. If the module is a driver for a hardware device – and most are – you can use parameters to tell the driver module what the device's address and irq are or set up any options which are private to that device. For example on one of my computers I have a sound card that includes a joystick port. The parameter

```
joystick=1
```

tells the driver module to switch the joystick port on.

Modules can make use of other modules. This is an example of part of the output from lsmod:

```
Module        Size    Used by    Not tainted
plip          10776   0    (unused)
parport_pc    17092   1    (autoclean)
parport       33184   1    [plip parport_pc]
```

The module parport – which provides basic parallel port functions – is used by the modules plip which uses the port for networking and parport_pc which uses it as a printer port.

Parport must be installed before either of the other two modules, and the other two must be removed before parport can be removed.

As root you can use three commands to manipulate modules.

• insmod – Installs a module. Type

```
insmod name param=value param=value...
```

filling in the name of the module you want to load and any parameters you want to give to it.

• rmmod – Removes a module. Type

```
rmmod name
```

• modprobe – Installs or removes a module, resolving dependencies as it goes. Use

```
modprobe name
```

to install a module and its dependencies and

```
modprobe -r name
```

to remove it.

Modprobe makes use of the files /etc/modules.conf and /lib/modules/(version)/modules.dep where (version) is your kernel version. The installation process normally sets up modules.conf, which tells modprobe which modules are drivers for which peripherals and how to load them.

Installation tries to identify each device and find the correct module for it. All chips that connect to the PCI bus, and many others, have some sort of readable identity which the installation program can use to identify the hardware. Unfortunately some chip manufacturers have been a little careless about identities and this does not always work. If you have a problem with a particular device, and you can find out – possibly by asking for help on a discussion group – which driver you should be using you can edit modules.conf to force Linux to load the correct driver.

When Linux is starting up it creates the modules.dep file – you will see the message 'Finding module dependencies:' while this is happening. In this file it puts a table of which modules make use of other ones. Modprobe uses this table to make sure, before it loads a module, that if the one being loaded needs other modules they are loaded first.

As an ordinary user – without root access – you can still use peripherals that need modular drivers.

Simply use a device. The kernel will notice that it has no driver and run modprobe to load one. The modules.conf file controls this process. For example the line

```
alias eth0 e100
```

on one of my computers tells modprobe that the correct driver for the eth0 Ethernet interface is a module called e100.

You can set Linux up to handle devices that the kernel does not know about. I have a driver which communicates with some programmable chips. To access it I have created a character device called /dev/xilinx with major number 122 and minor 0.

When an ordinary user tries to program a chip by writing to /dev/xilinx the kernel notices that it has no driver for this device, and that it has no idea what device 122 is anyway. So it labels the device 'char-major-122' and asks modprobe for help.

Modprobe looks in /etc/modules.conf and finds the line

```
alias char-major-122 xilinx
```

which tells it to look for a module called xilinx. Modprobe then looks in the standard place, which is /lib/modules, finds the module in a subdirectory and loads it.

The same works for block devices, except that the kernel asks for block-major-n instead.

When a module is loaded it fuses with the kernel, becomes part of the running system. It can use software within the kernel and the kernel can make use of it. For this to work properly the module has to be compiled to match a specific version of the kernel – in the same way that a key has to be cut to fit a specific lock. Since the source of most drivers (this is explained in the next chapter) is freely available this is not a problem, you can recompile any driver module in a few seconds.

Some hardware manufacturers do not want to release the source code of drivers for their devices, either because the code contains tricks they have invented, or because it gives away how their hardware improvements work. One way around this has been to create a driver which is in two parts. One module interacts with the kernel and is released as source. The other part – which is released as a binary module – operates the hardware and only interacts with the first module.

10

programming for beginners (optional)

In this chapter you will learn:

- what development tools are included with Linux and how to use them
- how to write programs that use the Graphical User Interface
- how to program with TCL, TK and Tix
- how to use Perl

All Linux distributions come with a variety of programming tools. You do not need to know anything about programming to make use of Linux, but learning some programming will empower you to do much more with the system.

This chapter will introduce you to the basics of programming. It will teach you how to create simple programs, and how to understand other people's.

10.1 Basic development tools

Programming languages are used to give instructions to computers. The actual instructions which the processor chip in your PC executes are complex, frequently obscure, patterns of binary digits. It is possible to write these instructions directly in binary, or indirectly using a special kind of programming language called assembly code. An assembler program – one is included with Linux as part of the gcc package – translates the lists of instruction names which you write into binary for the processor. Programming in assembly code is a specialized and highly skilled business, and is very rarely necessary.

For ordinary programming you can write your programs in either a compiled or an interpreted language. A compiled language is translated by a program called a compiler into instructions which the processor chip can understand. These instructions are then put in a separate executable binary file, which is read into memory and given to the processor when you run the program. The original file which you wrote, called the *source code,* is not needed to run the program.

To make a change to a compiled program you alter the source and recompile. Amending a binary after compilation is very difficult.

Most commercial software is distributed only as executable binary files. Linux, distributed under the GPL, comes with the source code. This is the meaning of the term 'open source'. Its value is that you can change any part of Linux, either because you have found and fixed a bug, or because you want it do do something different.

An interpreted language is understood by a program called an interpreter. This reads the program, either a little at a time or all at once, then works its way through, line by line, obeying the instructions it finds on each line. Some interpreters work by partially compiling the program first. Either way, an interpreter works on the source code – there is no binary file.

Linux normally comes with at least compilers for C, C++ and FORTRAN, and interpreters for TCL, Guile and Perl. The bash shell also works as an interpreter for its own scripting language.

If you want to learn a compiled language your first choice should be C. It is easy to master and so widely used as to be almost a standard.

You can develop a program in two ways. The classical method, which works on all Linux and UNIX variants, is to run the various development tools from the command line. This is much preferred by the older generation of programmers (including the author) who can drive the CLI far faster and more reliably than anything involving a mouse.

The tools which you can use from the command line include:

- Editors, such as emacs.
- Version control packages such as CVS.
- Compilers such as gcc and their associated programs.
- Make, which supervises the compilers.

CVS keeps track of which source files are needed to build which projects, what was changed when, and who made the changes. It keeps a 'repository' of files – not only the source code but lists of changes as well. You can 'checkout' any files you want to work on, make your changes and 'commit' the new version to the repository.

If two programmers check out the same file and make changes CVS is remarkably clever at reconciling the two versions.

You can also use CVS to 'tag' a particular version of your sources, for example you can use CVS to fix the sources that built a binary you have given to someone else. Then you can always use the tag to get back the exact sources from which that binary was built – a useful thing to do if the person with the binary complains of a problem.

Gcc – the C and C++ compiler – uses many dozens of options. You can ignore most of them if you want to compile a simple program. For example type

```
gcc -o fish fish.c
```

to compile the c source code in fish.c and end up with a binary in fish. You can then run the program by typing:

```
./fish
```

The make command is controlled by a file, usually called Makefile (note the capital M), in your current directory. This file contains a series of targets – files which will be created when you compile your program, and directions for building them. This is an extract from a real Makefile which builds a program called dw_cameras.

```
dw_cameras: dw_cameras.c font.h
        gcc -o dw_cameras dw_cameras.c -ljpeg -lm
```

The target is a file called dw_cameras – this is the binary executable. The colon after the name of the target indicates that the remaining things on the line are dependencies – files which contribute to the final binary.

Make will look at the timestamps on the dependencies and on the target. If the target is missing, or if any dependency has a later timestamp, Make runs the commands which then create the target.

The commands are on the lines following the target. They must be indented with a tab character, not with spaces. The command in the example compiles dw_cameras.c to make dw_cameras, adding in the maths library (-lm) and the jpeg image format library (-ljpeg).

The second way of developing a program is to use an *Integrated Development Environment* (IDE), such as the kdevelop package, which is included with some distributions. It combines editor, Make utility and debugger in one application.

IDEs work in terms of projects, rather than individual programs. A project is a collection of all the files needed to create a program and its associated documentation. An IDE can create a complete project, generating all the files, when you click on a menu item.

Kdevelop generates files with great zeal. If you ask it to create the simplest possible project – a program that prints 'Hello, world!' and does nothing else – it will create a project complete with skeleton HTML documentation and GPL licence. This is a total of 115 files and directories taking up 3.8 megabytes of disk space. The smallest properly commented and formatted version of the same program that I could contrive by the old method, using the CLI, is 87 bytes. On the other hand if I wanted to distribute the program to other users I would have to add most of the things that are in the `kdevelop` version.

Developing programs that use the GUI is much easier with an IDE such as `kdevelop`. GUI applications tend to include large quantities of very predictable code – tedious to write by hand but easy to generate automatically. You can create most of the code of the graphical part of a simple GUI application in a few minutes with `kdevelop`.

10.2 GUI applications and widget sets

The X-Windows system is only the bottom-most layer of the GUI. It can do simple things like writing text on the screen and drawing lines. To make it into a useful system, any programs you write must add another layer – they must have a way of drawing buttons, sliders, menus and all the things that make up a complete GUI.

The software to draw all of these things – often called widgets – is usually taken from a library. Over many years, several widget sets and the library code to draw them have been developed, first for UNIX, then for Linux.

Unfortunately not all of these have been free, open-source, software. The Athena widget set is one of the most basic, and is still used by some older programs. It was superceded by the Motif package. There is a free version of Motif called OpenMotif, and a free clone called Lesstif.

The Qt package, which includes a very good widget set, is sold by Trolltech AS, based in Oslo. A free version of Qt, which can be used in other free programs, is available for download from their site, http://www.trolltech.com.

Trolltech also supply a program called Designer which you can use to sketch a user interface with mouse and keyboard, and have the relevant code generated automatically. Designer and `kdevelop` are integrated – you can use Designer to create the GUI for `kdevelop` applications.

10.3 Serial interface

Your computer probably has at least two serial ports which you can use to communicate with modems, serial printers and other computers.

Linux keeps an internal list of serial ports. You can manipulate this list – at least for hardware that the kernel knows about – with the setserial command. For most standard hardware there is no need to do this, but if you have extra serial ports you can tell the kernel how to access them with setserial. You can use the /etc/rc.serial file described in Chapter 9 to do this.

There is a limit to the number of serial ports you can add to your computer if you use the old style of single and dual port cards – mainly because you run out of valid addresses and interrupt lines. If you need four or more extra ports you can use a multiport card. These cards commonly have between four and several dozen ports, and include a small, fast processor which looks after all the housekeeping tasks associated with the card. If the kernel knows about your multiport card the appropriate driver will be loaded automatically as the system starts up; if not, you may need to add a driver. If so, you may be able to download the driver from the card manufacturer's website, in which case it will come with installation instructions.

Every serial port, from the old-style simple ones to the most sophisticated multiport cards, has the same programming interface. They all support the read() and write() calls to transfer data, select() to test for the port being ready to transfer data and ioctl() to set the *baud rate*, character format and flow control. Because this interface is standard you can expect any software that works with one type of serial port to behave in the same way with another.

10.4 TCL, TK and tix

The Tool Command Language (TCL) is distributed free and is included in most distributions. You can learn more about it at http://www.scriptics.com. It is a scripting language which has a lot of useful features, particularly for manipulating text strings.

TK is an extension to TCL which lets you write scripts that use the GUI. You can display windows, put up dialogue boxes, add menus and make objects that can be dragged with the mouse. Tix extends TK by adding a number of extra widgets, including a very useful directory and file selection tool.

The TCL interpreter is designed to be combined with other programs to give them a ready-made command language. Alternatively there are three shell programs that work as a simple interface to the interpreter.

- The `tclsh` program is a basic, text-only shell that runs simple TCL scripts. It is a good way of trying out simple scripts.
- The windowing shell, `wish`, is similar to `tclsh`, but has the TK components built in. You can use it to create graphical applications.
- The `tixwish` shell is an enhanced form of `wish` which includes the `tix` extensions. Use it if you want the more complex widgets, the directory listboxes or anything else in the `tix` extensions.

The easiest way to begin using TCL is to try out a few commands with `tclsh`.

Type `tclsh` to start the shell. It will display a percent sign (%) to prompt you for a command.

The first command to try is `set`, which sets a variable to a value. It 'returns' the new value of the variable. Try this:

```
[unclebob@titania unclebob]$ tclsh
% set Jim 3
3
% set Fred 7
7
```

This has set the variable Jim to have the value 3 and Fred to have the value 7. Now we can do something with the variables.

```
% puts $Jim
3
```

The `puts` command prints its argument. The dollar sign ($) before Jim tells the TCL interpreter 'substitute the value of Jim here'.

```
% puts [ expr $Fred + $Jim ]
10
```

This is a slightly more complicated example. The `expr` command works out the value of the expression, after the interpreter has replaced $Fred and $Jim with their values. In this case it works out 7 + 3 = 10, this is the return value from the `expr` command. Because the command is in square brackets the interpreter then replaces it with its return value and finally gets around to executing the `puts` command – which, after all the substitutions, has been converted into

```
puts 10
```

which, as you would expect, prints the number 10.

TCL has some built-in commands that access files. The `glob` command makes a global directory search and returns the matching file names. I did this in a directory that contained all the files for a small website:

```
% glob *.html
SF.html index.html rfts.html ctts.html romance.html
sk.html 80footer.html darkness.html
```

The return value from the `glob` command is a TCL list containing all the matching file names, in this case the HTML files. Lists are one of the most useful things about TCL. They can hold any sort of data – even other lists – in order and they are very easy to manipulate.

For anything more complicated than the last example it is worth putting your commands in a script file. The file in this example is ~/bin/cat.tcl – remember that ~/bin is in your path, so files in it with the correct permissions can be used as commands.

```
#! /usr/bin/tclsh

set N 1
foreach File [ glob *.html ] {
    puts "$N. $File"
    incr N
}
```

Make the file executable by typing

```
chmod u+x ~/bin/cat.tcl
```

then type

```
./cat.tcl
```

to run your script. It will list the files that match the parameter to `glob`, and count them. The output will look something like this:

```
1. SF.html
2. index.html
3. rfts.html
...
```

When you run this script the `glob` is evaluated, and it returns a list of file names. The `foreach` command then executes everything between the braces, { and }, once for each item in the list, setting `File` to the value of each item in the list in turn.

Inside the braces are two commands. One prints the count and file name, the second increments the count.

The TK extension to TCL is among the simplest possible ways of
writing programs that use the GUI quickly. To see how quick it
is, start the windowing shell by typing

```
wish
```

with no options.

The shell will display % as a prompt, and a window will open.
This window, which is tersely named '.', just one dot, is the root
window on which the rest of a TK application is built.

Now put something in the window. Type

```
label .fred -text "Hello World"
```

to the shell. Note that the return value '.fred' is printed by the
shell. This has created an object – in this case a text label called
.fred. The next step is to place it somewhere in the window.
Type

```
pack .fred
```

and the 'pack' geometry manager will put it in the first available
space and resize the window around it.

Do this again with a second label

```
label .jim -text "Goodbye World!"
pack .jim
```

and the window will resize again around the two labels.

Try adding some user interaction. Type

```
button .eric -text "Please do not press this button"
.eric configure -command "puts \"Oh, no. Not again!\""
pack .eric
```

and a button will appear in the window. The button command
creates the button called .eric, but *it also creates a command
called .eric to let you do things to the button.*

The configure option changes anything that you could have set
with the command that created the button.

The button now has two parameters: the text it displays, and a
command that it executes when the button is pushed. Note that
the command contains a quoted string inside quotes, so the inner
quotes are *escaped* with the backslash (\) character to tell the
interpreter that they belong inside the outer quotes.

Click on the button. TK will execute the command you have associated with the button and you will see the message come out in the shell.

Wish can run a script from a file. Type this script into a file called ~/bin/colour.tcl, and use the command

chmod u+x ~/bin/colour.tcl

to make it executable.

```
#! /usr/bin/wish

# Simple wish demo

label .whatsit -text "Watch the colours"

frame .things -borderwidth 3 -relief ridge
button .things.r -text Red -command ".whatsit configure -fg red"
button .things.g -text Green -command ".whatsit configure -fg green"
button .things.b -text Blue -command ".whatsit configure -fg blue"

pack .whatsit .things
pack .things.r .things.g .things.b -side left
```

Now type ./colour.tcl to run the script. You will see a 'ridge' – a narrow raised border around the buttons. This is created by the parameters to the frame command.

The text message and the frame around the buttons are packed top to bottom in the window. The first pack command does this. Then the second pack command packs the buttons left to right inside the frame. The names of the buttons – .things.r, .things.g and .things.b – reflect the fact that they are part of the larger object called '.things'.

One big difference between tclsh and wish is that when a script run by tclsh reaches the end of the file the shell exits. With wish the script is executed to the end, setting up things that can happen later as it goes.

Once a wish script reaches the end, wish enters an event loop, where it sits waiting for incoming events, such as mouse clicks and keystrokes. When an event, such as a mouse click on a button, makes something happen in your program, the event loop runs a callback, such as the '.whatsit configure' commands in the example.

An application written with wish *contains only initialization and callbacks*, there is no 'ordinary' program at all.

10.5 Perl

Perl is a language in which you can write scripts. It has more features than the shell, but is neither as powerful nor as fast as C. Unlike a shell script, or TCL, a Perl program is compiled before execution. Because of this you cannot, for example, use commands that are created by text substitution as the program runs. This makes it slightly less powerful than TCL in some respects, but a great deal easier to use. When you try to run a Perl script it will either start or fail with a syntax error. A shell or TCL script may conceal a syntax error until that part of the program is run.

Perl's particular strength is in handling text. Its name *Practical Extraction and Report Language* comes from its original use – extracting information from large numbers of text files and formatting it in a readable fashion. It has built-in functions to search and sort through text, and it can convert arrays into lists and vice versa.

Perl has a number of ways of connecting to databases. It can also connect to the TK package, which is normally bundled with TCL, and use it to generate a graphical user interface. See the previous section for a description of TK.

Some parts of Linux itself are written in Perl, particularly scripts that convert data from one form to another, or configure new software when it is first installed.

Many CGI scripts – these are scripts which generate web pages dynamically – are written in Perl.

This is a simple demonstration program in Perl.

```perl
#! /usr/bin/perl

# Type in a month number ( 1 - 12 ) and
# this script will return
# the month name

@Months = qw ( January February March April May June
  July August September October November December ) ;

while ( 1 ) {
  print "Month number: " ;
  $N = <STDIN> ;

  if ( $N < 1 || $N > 12 ) { die "That's not a month." }
  print "$Months[ $N - 1 ]\n" ;
}
```

The first line after the comments creates a list of month names. The qw operator takes the month names, turns them into a list and places them in the array Months. The while statement then creates a loop in which the program prints a prompt and reads one line from standard input – note that <STDIN> behaves almost like a variable, you can read data simply by assigning from it. If the value read in is not a month number the script makes use of the die command to exit with an error message. If the month number is valid the script subtracts one (Months begin at 1, Perl arrays begin at zero) and uses it to find the month name in the array.

careers with linux

In this chapter you will learn:

- how to study for certification
- how to develop your career

Commercial organizations and some government departments are rapidly converting to Linux, in order to take advantage of higher reliability at lower cost.

If you want to make your career with Linux you can either choose formal training with certification, or an informal, hands-on approach.

I normally avoid making predictions, at least until after the event. In this case my best guess is that Linux will increasingly be adopted by major concerns, and a side-effect of this will be increasing significance of formal qualifications over the next decade.

Linux – in common with all open-source software – lends itself to informal learning by people who are interested enough to go and look things up for themselves. Fortunately the designers of the certification programmes have recognized this.

11.1 Certification

The *Linux Professional Institute* (LPI) at http://www.lpi.org/ issue certifications which are not specific to distributions and which are rapidly gaining acceptance.

Red Hat Corporation operate a formal certification programme, leading to either the *Red Hat Certified Engineer* (RHCE) or *Red Hat Certified Technician* (RHCT) qualifications. Both of these are given after both a practical and a written exam. The RHCE indicates your ability to set up a network, making the relevant engineering decisions. The RHCT is the lesser qualification, showing that you know how to maintain and extend a working system.

Because these qualifications are 'performance-based' – only given after a practical examination – they are becoming accepted as proof that you can really make a system work.

The practical examination is more searching than a simple multiple-choice test; most candidates who fail the practical pass the written exam. This has one major advantage – if you can pass the RHCE tests it is clear that you know what you are doing.

There are several courses leading to the RHCE and RHCT qualifications. Before parting with money make sure that any course you are thinking of taking is approved by Red Hat as meeting the requirements of their current examination.

The course designers accept that students will come to the courses with differing levels of knowledge. There are 'fast track' options you can choose if you have already built up some experience with Linux.

You will also find some courses that deal with specific aspects of Linux. These usually lead to a course completion certificate. Employers often send their staff on these courses, and expect the certificate as proof that the student has made satisfactory progress.

Informal training is sometimes organized by LUGs. While this leads to no recognizable qualification it has the huge advantage that it is usually free.

1.2 Career development

The IT industry, of which Linux is a part, regularly lurches between boom and total collapse. The availability of Linux jobs is affected by this cycle. The best strategy is to plan for a wait of many months before your ideal opening presents itself. If you want to use an agency make sure that you pick one that has some idea of what Linux is or you may waste a great deal of your time and everyone else's – weeding out unsuitable vacancies.

Acquiring formal Linux skills, even possessing informal skills garnered from using Linux, will improve your employment prospects. There is some statistical evidence that Linux skills, particularly when backed up by a formal certification, have a positive effect on salaries.

There is one small pitfall here, and a warning to employers. If you are the only person in an organization with Linux skills the management will assume that you are on call all day and night throughout the whole year. I have once surfaced from a scuba dive to be presented with a fax asking for help with what turned out to be a fairly trivial problem.

Linux skills are best developed by using them. If you have an idea for something that might be done, or you want to find out how some feature works – try it. I have always allocated a proportion of my time to what I called *piano practice* – writing small and possibly useless programs to test concepts. I have explored most of the quieter backwaters of the system in this way.

12

advanced topics (optional)

In this chapter you will learn:

- how to install Linux on an embedded processor
- how to obtain real-time performance from Linux
- how to configure and compile the kernel
- how to create your own software packages

This chapter describes some interesting things that you can do with Linux. Some of these things need hardware that is not found in ordinary desktop computers, so you may not be able to try all of these out for yourself.

12.1 Embedded Linux

The chip that is buried away inside a video recorder or a mobile phone to scan the keyboard, work the display and control the appliance itself is called an embedded processor.

For many years embedded processors were mainly programmed in assembler and used very small amounts of memory. Over the past few years memory has become much cheaper and smaller, while the functions demanded from an embedded processor have grown. There is now a trend towards embedded processors using minimal versions of Linux. While this imposes a penalty on the system design – the kernel occupies several megabytes – the benefits in reduced development cost and time to market usually more than outweigh the penalties. Using Linux on an embedded processor has the enormous advantage of providing a scheduler, filesystem support and networking at minimal cost.

There are a number of Linux distributions designed specifically for embedded processors. You can find typical examples of these at http://www.mvista.com/, http://www.denx.de/ and http://www.redhat.com/embedded/.

An embedded distribution has to be able to run without a hard-disk drive attached to the processor. There are two ways it can do this. Either it can create an image of a disk in RAM, or it can make use of a hard disk on another machine by mounting its root filesystem over NFS at an early point in the boot sequence, in exactly the same way that a diskless workstation makes use of a disk on another machine.

Embedded processors commonly start up by using a bootstrap program to load a compressed kernel from memory whose contents cannot be changed by the running system. This *Read-Only Memory* (ROM) exists in several forms. Current practice is to use *Electrically Erasable Programmable Read-Only Memory* (EEPROM) which can be programmed 'in circuit' – with the memory chips physically attached to the processor board. At the same time the bootstrap loads a compressed initial ramdisk.

When the kernel starts up it first decompresses itself and the ramdisk. It then mounts the ramdisk – which is only a filesystem held in an area of RAM rather than on a disk – as the root directory. On a conventional system the ramdisk contains the files needed to get the system started. An embedded processor often has a complete system in a much bigger ramdisk.

The Embedded Linux Portal site at http://www.linux devices.com/ has a lot of information about embedded Linux.

Before starting work on an embedded system you can get some experience of this sort of programming, even develop much of the software you will use in the real system, by working with an embeddable processor board.

TQ Components http://www.tq-components.com/ are one of several companies that make a range of these boards. A 'starter kit' containing a processor board and everything needed to get it working costs a little less than a basic desktop computer.

To use it you will need another Linux machine to use as the development workstation, and some means of communicating with the board, such as a serial connection or a LAN.

Denx Software Engineering http://www.denx.de/ supplies a distribution of Linux which runs on many of these embeddable boards. This includes a version of the kernel tailored for embedded use, and cross-compilers that you can use to generate code for the embedded processor from your PC.

12.2 Real-time Linux

The term 'real time' is intended to describe computing that keeps up with events happening in the real world. The variety of external events means that 'real time' can imply anything from 'The computer ought to respond before the customer loses patience' to 'The machine stops working if we do not produce a result within one ten-thousandth of a second'. Often the shorter the time the computer has to respond the more disastrous the results if it does not.

The Linux kernel was not originally intended for real-time use. Some operations, particularly those which involve allocating or freeing memory, can take over a second. Linux allows tasks to be pre-empted – if a higher-priority task needs to run, a lower priority one can be halted. However, the kernel itself is not pre emptable. If a lower-priority task has, for example, requested more memory, and the kernel has wandered off to do a leisurely sift through the memory pool, the higher-priority task will not get a chance to run until the kernel finishes its interesting diversion. Meanwhile, deprived of commands, something catastrophic may have happened to the hardware your computer is controlling.

The delay between an external event happening and the kernel giving control to the task that deals with it is called the *latency*. Reducing latency is a prerequisite for making Linux work in critical real-time applications.

Low-latency versions of the kernel are available, for example Monta Vista at http://www.mvista.com have a commercial version. These depend on a complex series of modifications known as 'the low-latency patch' which make the kernel break up long operations into a series of short ones.

There is an alternative solution called 'The Love Patch' after its inventor, Robert M. Love. This takes advantage of the way in which the kernel runs on computers with more than one processor. On multiprocessor systems the kernel running on one processor can pre-empt the kernel on another. The Love patch extends this to allow a high-priority task to pre-empt the kernel. The Love patch is being integrated into the kernel itself, and will probably be a standard feature when the version 2.6 kernel is released.

FSM labs, http://www.fsmlabs.com/, distribute both free and commercial versions of RTLinux. The RTLinux kernel has two schedulers, a very fast one to run real-time code, and the normal Linux scheduler that runs when the fast one has nothing to do. This is an effective way of running time-critical code without disrupting normal tasks. Real-time code running under the fast scheduler does not have access to all the system calls – this does not matter for almost all real-time applications.

Writing a real-time application for Linux, particularly if you already have some experience of real-time computing, is entirely straightforward. These are the steps involved in designing a typical application:

1. Find out exactly what hardware you are using, and how much data has to be read from or written to each interface.
2. Investigate how much computation you need to do to work out what is to be written to the interfaces.
3. Make a list of all the things your application must do. Divide it into things that absolutely must be done on time, and things that can be deferred without causing a disaster.

4 Decide how the time-critical and non-critical sections of your application will communicate. Make sure that this cannot hold up the time-critical section.

12.3 Configuring and compiling the kernel

The Linux kernel itself is just another program. It may well be the largest one you will ever come across – but it can be modified and rebuilt with exactly the same tools as any other program.

Because the kernel is so large and complex it comes equipped with some programs to simplify the process of creating the kernel binary.

The kernel-building process – compiling, linking and, where necessary, compressing the program components – is largely automatic. In this section I will describe it briefly. Once you have built a kernel you will find that the documentation becomes easy to understand, and you will be able to build non-standard kernels if you need them.

The things you can do if you rebuild the kernel are:

- Tune the kernel to make more efficient use of the hardware in your computer.
- Apply patches to correct kernel problems or add new features.
- Add diagnostic printouts to help you identify problems.

In theory you might be able to find and fix a kernel bug yourself, but in practice bugs in new versions of the kernel are very quickly hunted to extinction – there are precious few left for you to stalk by the time a kernel finds its way onto a distribution disk.

The kernel source files are usually in /usr/src/linux and its subdirectories. This is normally a symbolic link to the current version, which will be a directory with a name such as /usr/src/linux-2.4.20-8 containing the actual files.

Building the kernel is controlled by the file /usr/src /linux/.config, which is created when you configure the kernel.

You can use several programs to create this file. You may also find some useful sample configurations in /usr/src/linux /configs/.

Before building the kernel you should log in as root, and change to the /usr/src/linux/ directory.

The command

```
make oldconfig
```

will try to create a `.config` file from the installed system. You may need to run this command twice. You can then edit the configuration if necessary by typing

```
make xconfig
```

which will give you a profusion of clickable options. You can choose the 'y' (Yes) button for an option to have it built into the kernel, 'n' to leave it out or 'm' to have it built as a module that can be loaded by the running kernel.

The next step is to type

```
make dep
```

which works its way through the entire kernel finding *dependencies*, information about source files which need other files to build them.

If this step completes correctly you can build the kernel itself. Type

```
make bzImage
```

and, unless something goes wrong at once, make yourself a cup of tea. The build process will churn away for many minutes, finally creating a file containing a loadable image of the resident part of the kernel.

Before going any further make sure that you can still get your system to come up even if you wreck the installed kernel. Use the `mkbootdisk` command (the command may be different on some distributions) to create an emergency reboot floppy.

The README file in the kernel sources tells you to build the loadable modules next. However this may not work if the kernel you are building is not the same version as the one you are running. The problem is that scripts may try to build the loadable modules using information from the installed kernel and fail because of various incompatibilities. If this happens you will need to install the kernel you have just built with

```
make install
```

before building the modules with

```
make modules
```

which can take even longer than building the resident portion.

By installing the new kernel you should not damage the old one – they should have different version numbers. In the unlikely event that something goes wrong and you make your system inoperable, you can recover the situation by booting from your recovery floppy, then copying the files on the floppy back into the /boot directory. You may need to reinstall your boot loader as well – follow the instructions in Chapter 8.

Some distributions make use of the EXTRAVERSION parameter to differentiate a kernel which you have built by appending the word 'custom' or similar to the version number. Look in /usr/src/linux/Makefile to see if your distribution uses this facility.

Now type

```
make modules_install
```

to copy the modules you have created into /lib/modules.

Installing the kernel should have rebuilt the initial ramdisk as well. However, it may have been rebuilt with modules from the old kernel, so it is worth doing

```
make install
```

again at this point to force the current modules into the initial ramdisk.

Adjust your boot loader (see Chapter 8) to offer your new kernel as a boot option. This happens automatically when you install the kernel with some distributions.

You can now reboot your machine and, if all has gone well, it will come up running your new kernel. If not, examine any error messages carefully. Common reasons for a new kernel not starting are:

- Boot loader incorrectly set up. It may be trying to load the kernel from the wrong file, or a kernel and an initial ramdisk that are not the same version.

- Kernel built for wrong hardware. Your kernel may be trying to run code built for a Pentium on an old 486.

- Incorrect built-in driver. If you compile in a driver for hardware that is not installed on your machine you may produce a kernel that starts and then crashes at once.

Once your new kernel is running you can begin to customize it.

Begin by trying the effect of changing an option and seeing what happens. The sequence of commands is:

```
make xconfig
make dep
make bzImage
make modules
make modules_install
```

Once you have done this you can do anything with the kernel. In particular, you can install kernel patches.

An example of a kernel patch is shown in Figure 12.1. This patch was written by Steve Purcell, to whom I am indebted for his kind permission to include it in this book.

This patch enables the kernel to communicate correctly with the Freecom FS-1 CD recorder. This drive makes a slightly unusual response to the USB INQUIRY command. The patch enables Linux to recognize the drive correctly from this response.

The patch was created by editing a new copy of the kernel source to fix the problem, then using the `diff` command to make a list of the changes. The output of `diff`, which is the patch, is the text in the figure.

The patch indicates that three files, `unusual_devs.h`, `usb.c` and `usb.h` were modified. Within each file it gives a rough location, on the lines beginning `@@`, of the change. Then it shows a sample of unaltered code, the new code marked with '+' at the beginnings of lines, and another short unaltered section. Deleted lines (there are none in the example) would be marked with '-' at the beginning of the line.

The `patch` command can make the same change to another set of source files by reading the patch and making edits.

This works in most cases even if the code being patched is not quite the same as the version on which the patch was generated. Patch deals with this in a very intelligent way, trying to match the samples of unaltered code to the file that it is editing, and adjusting the point at which it inserts or deletes code to match.

This patch was generated on kernel version 2.4.21. I put it in a file called `fs1patch` in the kernel source and applied it successfully to `2.4.20` by using these commands:

```
cd /usr/src/linux-2.4.20-13.9/
patch -b -p1 -F 5 <fs1patch
```

```
diff -Naur kernel-source-2.4.21-pre3/drivers/usb/storage/unusual_devs.h kernel-source-2.4.21-pre3.patched/drivers/usb/storage/unusual_devs.h
--- kernel-source-2.4.21-pre3/drivers/usb/storage/unusual_devs.h 2003-01-24 13:53:31.000000000 +0100
+++ kernel-source-2.4.21-pre3.patched/drivers/usb/storage/unusual_devs.h 2003-01-24 13:01:09.000000000 +0100
@@ -411,6 +411;11 @@
                US_SC_QIC, US_PR_FREECOM, freecom_init, 0),

 #endif

+UNUSUAL_DEV( 0x07ab, 0xfc03, 0x0000, 0x9999,
+       &quot;Freecom&quot;,
+       &quot;USB FS-1 CD-RW&quot;,
+       US_SC_8020, US_PR_BULK, NULL, US_FL_INQUIRY_CD),
+
 UNUSUAL_DEV( 0x07af, 0x0004, 0x0100, 0x0133,
        &quot;Microtech&quot;,
        &quot;USB-SCSI-DB25&quot;,
diff -Naur kernel-source-2.4.21-pre3/drivers/usb/storage/usb.c kernel-source-2.4.21-pre3.patched/drivers/usb/storage/usb.c
--- kernel-source-2.4.21-pre3/drivers/usb/storage/usb.c 2002-11-29 17:31:59.000000000 +0100
+++ kernel-source-2.4.21-pre3.patched/drivers/usb/storage/usb.c 2003-01-24 12:48:51.000000000 +0100
@@ -453,6 +453,15 @@
                US_DEBUGP(&quot;Faking INQUIRY command\n&quot;);
                fill_inquiry_response(us, data_ptr, 36);
                us-&gt;srb-&gt;result = GOOD &lt;&lt; 1;
+       } else if ((us-&gt;srb-&gt;cmnd[0] == INQUIRY) &amp;&amp;
+                  (us-&gt;flags &amp; US_FL_FIX_INQUIRY_CD)) {
+               unsigned char data_ptr[36] = {
+                       0x05, 0x80, 0x02, 0x02,
+                       0x1F, 0x00, 0x00, 0x00};
+
+               US_DEBUGP(&quot;Faking INQUIRY command for CD-ROM\n&quot;);
+               fill_inquiry_response(us, data_ptr, 36);
+               us-&gt;srb-&gt;result = GOOD &lt;&lt; 1;
+
        } else {
                /* we've got a command, let's do it! */
                US_DEBUGP(us,stor_show_command(us-&gt;srb));
diff -Naur kernel-source-2.4.21-pre3/drivers/usb/storage/usb.h kernel-source-2.4.21-pre3.patched/drivers/usb/storage/usb.h
--- kernel-source-2.4.21-pre3/drivers/usb/storage/usb.h 2002-11-29 17:32:19.000000000 +0100
+++ kernel-source-2.4.21-pre3.patched/drivers/usb/storage/usb.h 2003-01-24 13:01:07.000000000 +0100
@@ -101,6 +101,8 @@
 #define US_FL_IGNORE_SER        0x00000010  /* Ignore the serial number given */
 #define US_FL_SCM_MULT_TARG     0x00000020  /* supports multiple targets */
 #define US_FL_FIX_INQUIRY       0x00000040  /* INQUIRY response needs fixing */
+#define US_FL_FIX_INQUIRY_CD    0x00000080  /* INQUIRY response needs fixing for CD
+ROM */

 #define USB_STOR_STRING_LEN 32
```

Figure 12.1 A kernel patch

The -b option makes patch keep a backup copy of the unchanged files. Because the name of the directory in which I was applying the patch was not the same as the directory where the patch was created I used the -p1 option to remove the first part of the path – everything up to the first slash – from the paths in the patch. Setting -F 5 increases the 'fuzz', the extent to which patch will accept source files that do not correspond exactly with the patch.

I added the --dummy-run option the first time I tried to apply the patch. This told me that the patch would work without actually changing anything. When I had all the other parameters right I removed this option.

Then I rebuilt the modules – the patch does not affect the resident kernel. Finally I used rmmod to unload the old versions of the modules, plugged in the drive and everything worked.

Installing a kernel patch is probably the most complex thing you will ever do with Linux unless you decide to work on the kernel yourself. Once you have learned how to apply kernel patches you can consider yourself a fully fledged member of the Linux community. You can handle any problem that anyone else has solved by taking their solution and applying it to your kernel.

12.4 Creating packages

There are several package managers which run on Linux. The one you are most likely to use is the *RedHat Package Manager* (RPM). This program installs packages of files onto the system, maintains them, and can uninstall them. The packages RPM uses are held in files with the file type .rpm, such as designtools.rpm. Information about the package is usually built into the file name like this:

```
kamera-3.0.3-3.i386.rpm
```

This file is the package called kamera, version 3.0.3, build 3 for Intel 386 family processors.

An RPM package is an archive containing the files, and a header describing them. The rpm program installs a package by copying the files from the archive to their correct locations in your file tree and then making a note in its database of which files it has installed.

The rpm database contains information about each file installed and, because it is writable only by root, you can at any time verify a package to see if all its files still match their database entries. A file which does not match is not automatic evidence of the system having been tampered with – some files are legitimately changed by the package itself.

Because rpm knows which files each package contains it can often cleanly erase a package, leaving nothing behind.

Much software that runs on Linux is portable between several different operating systems. This sort of software is often distributed as a tarball, an archive made with the tar program and usually compressed with gzip.

You can turn your own software into rpms with the rpmbuild program – this used to be a part of rpm itself. Rpmbuild normally expects to convert a tarball into an rpm, so the easiest way to make something you have written into an rpm is to start off by making a tarball. Figure 12.2 is a map of the routes by which the different file formats can be converted into one another.

I have written a program called tsplit which splits up long files. I regularly use it to split a full backup of this computer over five CDs.

To make tsplit into an rpm needs only four files.

1 tsplit.c   This is the source code of the program.
2 tsplit.1   The man page for the program.
3 Makefile   The instructions for building the program.
4 tsplit-1.0.3-1.spec   The instructions for building the rpm.

You can make a man page for your program by creating a text file formatted in the way described in the man page 'howto', available on http://www.linux.org. Your manual page will be formatted for display or printing by a program called groff – or one of its relatives. These programs turn simple commands that you put in the text file into various kinds of formatting.

You can display the full list of formatting commands by typing this command:

```
man 7 groff_man
```

The version number of the package, 1.0.3-1 is built into the file name of the spec file, and nowhere else.

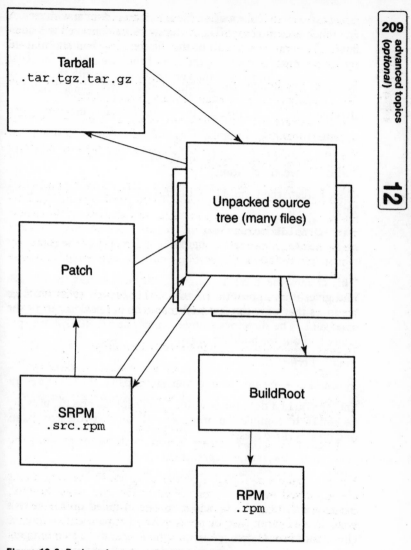

Figure 12.2 Package formats and build sequences

The easy way to make a spec file is to start editing it with emacs in your source directory. The current version of emacs will automatically create almost all of the file for you. You can find the full instructions for writing the rest of the spec file in the RPM howto. Be careful to read the version that goes with the copy of RPM you have, some steps in the process have changed recently.

To create the .rpm I first put the source files in a directory called

```
/home/unclebob/tsplit-1.0.3/
```

the last part of the name must match the package and the tarball we are creating.

Next I create the tarball with this command (it should all be on one line).

```
tar -C /oldhome/unclebob/ -cvzf
    /usr/src/redhat/SOURCES/tsplit-1.0.3.tar.gz
    tsplit-1.0.3
```

This creates the tarball in /usr/src/redhat/SOURCES, and gives it an appropriate name. Using the -C option to tar arranges that only the last path name component is put in the tarball. The directories under /usr/src/REDHAT are specially laid out for building rpms.

Finally I type

```
rpmbuild --clean -ta SOURCES/tsplit-1.0.3.tar.gz
```

and rpmbuild does the rest. It unpacks my tarball, uses my makefile to compile the program and compress the man page, and creates three files:

```
/usr/src/redhat/RPMS/i386/tsplit-1.0.3-1.i386.rpm
/usr/src/redhat/RPMS/i386/tsplit-debuginfo-1.0.3-1.i386.rpm
/usr/src/redhat/SRPMS/tsplit-1.0.3-1.src.rpm
```

These are the rpm itself, which can be installed on the system with the -i option to rpm, or sent over the internet to someone else, a tiny rpm of debugging information, and the source rpm.

The source rpm contains the tarball. You can, from the source rpm, repeat the entire build process.

If you are given a program in the form of a tarball you can try to turn it into an rpm in the same way. This may not always work, the program you have been given may have been developed on a different system and need some small tweaks to work with Linux.

The tidy way to deal with this is to unpack the `tarball` twice into two directories with slightly different names, fix the problem (sometimes easier said than done) and use the `diff` program to make a list of your changes. This list is known as a patch – I mentioned patching in an earlier section.

Now when you build the `rpm` you simply mention the patch in your `spec` file and `rpmbuild` will apply the patch.

taking it further

You now know enough about Linux to set up, use, secure and troubleshoot a Linux system.

Linux is a huge and rapidly growing world, through which you are ready to embark on an endlessly fascinating voyage of discovery. Here are some useful sources of information to help you find your way.

Distribution manufacturers

Debian	http://www.debian.org/
Gentoo	http://www.gentoo.org/
Knoppix	http://www.knopper.net/knoppix/index-en.html
Lindows	http://www.lindows.com/
Mandrake	http://www.mandrakesoft.com/
Red Hat	http://www.redhat.com/
Slackware	http://www.slackware.com/
SuSE	http://www.suse.com/

Other organizations

Linux Online http://www.linux.org/

Free Software Foundation and GNU Project
http://www.gnu.org/

X-Windows http://www.xfree.org/ and http://www.x.org/

Rpmfind, huge free software collection
http://www.rpmfind.net

ALSA (audio) project http://www.alsa-project.org/

Universal Serial Bus project
http://www.linux-usb.org/

High performance graphics http://www.opengl.org/

Video for Linux – TV cards and webcams
http://www.exploits.org/v4l/

Linux on laptops http://www.linux-laptop.net/

Application programs

CUPS (Printing)	http://www.cups.org/
OpenOffice	http://www.openoffice.org/
Gimp	http://www.gimp.org/
Gphoto	http://www.gphoto.org/
Xephem	http://www.clearskyinstitute.com/
Samba	http://www.samba.org/
SQL	http://www.postgresql.com/
	http://www.mysql.com/

Just for fun

Source of information about games, links to downloads
http://www.linuxgames.com/

Certification

Red Hat	https://www.redhat.com/training/rhce/courses/
LPI	http://www.lpi.org/

Books for Linux users

Linux in a Nutshell (4th Edition) by Ellen Siever, Aaron Weber, Stephen Figgins (Editors). (O'Reilly, 2003, ISBN: 0596004826) A useful reference to commands and utilities.

Running Linux (4th Edition) by Matt Welsh, Lar Kaufman, Matthias Kalle Dalheimer, Terry Dawson. (O'Reilly, 2002, ISBN: 0596002726)
Explains how much of the system works.

Books on programming

Learning Perl (3rd Edition) by Randal L. Schwartz, Tom Phoeenix. (O'Reilly, 2001, ISBN: 0596001320)
This is a useful introduction to the Perl language.

Linux Device Drivers (2nd Edition) by Alessandro Rubini, Jonathan Corbet. (O'Reilly, 2001 ISBN: 0596000081)
This book not only covers how to write device drivers but explains some of how the Linux kernel works. If you want to add new hardware to a Linux machine this book will guide you through the driver-writing process. Note that the first edition does not cover the current kernel.

PostScript® Language Tutorial and Cookbook by Adobe Systems Inc. (Addison-Wesley, 1985, ISBN: 0201101793)
This book explains the PostScript language which is used by Linux for printing. It shows you how to create printed output from your own programs.

Programming with Qt (2nd Edition) by Matthias Kalle Dalheimer. (O'Reilly, 2002, ISBN: 0596000642)
This is an introduction to Qt which will help you to write applications that use the GUI.

Linux Kernel Internals (2nd Edition) by Michael Beck (Editor) (Addison-Wesley, 1997, ISBN: 0201331438)
A more advanced guide to the internal workings of the Linux kernel.

Learning GNU Emacs, (2nd Edition) by Debra Cameron, Bill Rosenblatt, Eric S. Raymond. (O'Reilly, 1996, ISBN 1565921526)
This book will help if you want to make use of emacs. It covers editing and more advanced topics, such as using emacs as a mailer and newsreader.

Practical Programming in Tcl and Tk (4th Edition) by Brent Welch, Jeffrey Hobbs, Ken Jones. (Prentice Hall, 2003 ISBN 0130385603)

A practical introduction and useful reference, this book will enable you to make effective use of TCL and TK.

The best way to go on learning is to use Linux. Play the games, send someone an encouraging e-mail, participate in online discussions. Try your hand at writing scripts, draw a picture with Gimp, make a database of your favourite restaurants. Be prepared to experiment – Linux will often surprise you with a new and exciting feature.

You will discover all sorts of interesting things as you go on. Share your new knowledge, swap ideas with other Linux users and above all enjoy what you do.

glossary

absolute path	Description of how to find a file that is independent of the current directory.
always on	A network connection that does not depend on dialling a phone call.
bandwidth	Measure of the speed at which data can be transferred. Derived from radio practice this use of the word is not strictly correct.
baud rate	The rate, in bits per second, at which an interface sends data. The useful transfer rate is slower as not all bits contain data.
binary	A number system that uses the digits 0 and 1. Any data other than human-readable text.
BIOS	Basic Input/Output System.
bit	A binary digit, 0 or 1.
boot loader	The program that runs when you start your computer. It loads the operating system.
bootstrap	The process of loading an operating system. Because this has to be done before the drivers which know how to load a program from disk are loaded this operation is analogous to lifting yourself by pulling your own bootstraps.
builtin	A command which is part of a shell, as opposed to a command which is a separate program.

burning	Making an unchangeable recording of data, for example on a CDROM or in a read-only memory chip.
client	A program that makes use of something, such as shared files or a printer, provided by a server.
display manager	The program you talk to when you log in on a graphical screen. It also keeps track of your session.
escape	Mark as not having its usual meaning. For example the character * usually means 'Substitute all file names here.' But the asterisk can be escaped with a backslash, so * means 'put just an * here.'
executable	Something that can be understood as instructions by the computer.
expansion	Replacing a marker with data, for example replacing * with a list of files.
FAT	File Allocation Table, the system used by MS-DOS.
file tree	The system of directories that contains every file a Linux machine can access.
full backup	A backup of all the information in a disk partition.
gateway	A computer that forwards information from one network segment to another, or to the rest of the world.
graphical front end	A program that gives a point-and-click interface to something that would normally be done by typing commands
hexadecimal	A number system that uses base 16, written with digits 0–9 and A–F or a–f.
HFS	Hierarchical File System, the system used by Apple.
HPFS	High Performance File System.
HTML	HyperText Markup Language.
IDE	Integrated Drive Electronics.
incremental backup	Backup of all files changed since a particular date and time.
IP address	A set of numbers which identify one

	interface on a network or network segment.
ISP	Internet Service Provider.
latency	The time it takes a computer to respond to an external event.
major number	A number which identifies a device driver and connects it to an entry in /dev.
minor number	A number which identifies one particular device out of several similar ones.
mount point	A directory which is used as a place to attach a new file system to an existing one.
mount	Attach a filesystem – such as a disk – to a file tree, making it visible to the users.
noexec	An option which, when set on a filesystem, prevents Linux running any programs from that filesystem.
null string	A text string that contains no characters. The notation " ", quotes with nothing between them, is often used to indicate that a parameter is a null string.
option	Characters written after a CLI command which give additional instructions to the command, usually marked with one or two hyphens.
parameter	Characters written after a command to give it information; compare *option*.
path	A description of where to find a file, either absolutely or relative to the current directory.
permissions	Flags set on a file or directory to indicate who may read or write it.
PCI	Peripheral Component Interconnect.
PDF	Adobe's Portable Document Format, readable with Acrobat.
PPP	Point to Point Protocol.
prompt	Anything the computer displays to tell you that it is waiting for input.
protocol	A set of rules for how a particular type

	of data is sent from one machine to another.
pseudo user	A user identity, such as 'the web server', which is used to run programs but does not correspond to a real person.
Random Access Memory	Memory used to hold the programs and data your computer is actually working on, so called because it can be accessed in any order.
Read Only Memory	Memory that cannot be changed by the normal operation of your computer. Commonly used to hold instructions telling your computer how to start up when it is switched on.
redirect	To send data to a different place, for example to send something that would normally be seen on the screen to a printer.
relative path	A description of where a file is written as a route from the current directory to the file.
rescue system	A version of Linux that is started up to deal with a particular problem.
root	The person who has the privileges to be able to change anything on a Linux system.
root directory	The directory, written as a single slash character, that contains every other file and directory known to a Linux system. Do not confuse this with root's home directory, which is /root.
root squash	An NFS server which receives a request from a user on another machine who claims to be logged in as root can 'squash' the request, removing the root privileges.
router	A machine that redirects packets from one network segment to another.
RPC	Remote Procedure Call.
SCSI	Small Computer System Interface.

segment	One part of a network comprising computers that can communicate directly, not via a router.
server	A computer that provides a service, such as printing or handing out web pages, used by other machines.
source	The readable text form of a program used by programmers to work on it.
special file	A directory entry that represents something other than a file or directory. Special files are commonly used to access hardware devices such as disk drives and printer ports.
standard error	The stream on which a program puts out messages about errors, progress or anything else it needs to tell the operator.
standard input	The main input to a program, often the keyboard.
standard output	The main output from a program, often the screen.
symbolic link	A directory entry that points to another directory entry, rather than directly to a file.
text installation	Installing Linux without the GUI.
TCP/IP	Transmission Control Protocol/Internet Protocol.
Time To Live	The number of times a packet may be forwarded across networks without being discarded as undeliverable.
tunnel	To pass something through a firewall or another protocol without understanding it.
unicode	A method of encoding text which can handle multiple alphabets used by different languages.
UNIX	An older system from which some of the features of Linux are derived.
unmount	Reverse the action of mount, remove a filesystem from the tree.
URL	Uniform Resource Locator.
USB	Universal Serial Bus.
user	An ordinary person who uses Linux and has no special privileges.

vector graphics	A way of describing graphics in terms of coordinates. Vector graphics take no notice of how the display device works, and can be scaled without loss of quality.
VGA	Video Graphics Array.
visual	A means of connecting to a display and information about what that display can do.
working directory	Directory containing the files you are currently using.
zipfile	An archive file created with the zip program.

ADSL **101**
applications
    Apache **129**
    Applix **58**
    astronomy **67**
    CD mastering **67**
    cdrecord **68**
    CVS **185**
    Cygwin **114**
    digital photography
        66
    Evolution **61**
    Gimp **63**
    GnuCash **62**
    Imagemagick **65**
    kdevelop **186**
    Leafnode **134**
    Mars **119**
    MrProject **62**
    Netatalk **119**
    Office **52**, **117**
    pppd **123**
    presentation **54**
    Rosegarden **69**
    Samba **114**
    scanners **65**
    spreadsheet **54**
    Squid **140**
    Timidity **70**
    vector graphics **65**
    web browsers **54**,
        72
ASCII **25**
authentication **102**

backups
    automatic **147**
    media **149**
    offsite **153**
    other systems **148**
    planning **147**, **152**
    restoring from **162**
    software **145**
    timestamps **165**
    with tar **151**
bash **31**
binary **24**
BIOS **16**
boot loaders
    GRUB **16**
    LILO **16**

certification **196**
CGI **129**
command parameters **80**
commands
    apt-get **20**, **70**
    arp **108**
    cat **36**
    cd **36**
    cp **35**
    createdb **59**
    createuser **59**
    dos2unix **117**
    dpkg-reconfigure **20**
    dropdb **59**
    dropuser **59**
    echo **31**
    ethereal **106**

fuser **38**
ggv **88**
gnome-session **47**
gv **88**
info **34**
insmod **180**
ln **35**
lpadmin **85**
lpc **85**
lpr **84**
lprm **85**
ls **29**
make **186**
man **34**
mkbootdisk **203**
mkdir **36**
mkfs **42**
mkisofs **68**
mknod **43**
modprobe **180**
mount **37**
mv **35**
ping **103**
playwave **70**
pwd **36**
rm **35**
rmdir **36**
rmmod **180**
route **96**, **107**
rpm **144**
rpmbuild **208**
rsh **120**
smbclient **115**
smbmount **116**
sox **70**
ssh **121**
startx **15**, **26**
sync **177**
tcpdump **106**
telinit **45**
telnet **119**
traceroute **104**
umount **38**
unix2dos **117**
who **27**
xconsole **124**
xdpyinfo **49**
xhost **45**

xinit **46**
xmtr **106**
yast **20**
comments **79**
compiler **184**
Crontab **81**
CUPS **84**

data sources **55**
databases
    Adabas **56**
    address book **57**
    connecting to OpenOffice **61**
    dBase **52**, **56**
    JDBC **56**
    MySQL **60**
    ODBC **56**, **60**
    PostgreSQL **59**
    spreadsheet **56**
    SQL **52**, **58**
    tables **55**
datagram **94**
demand dialling **124**
desktops **49**
directories
    / **27**
    /dev **43**
diskless workstations **111**
disks
    cylinders **13**
    emergency boot **11**
    geometry **14**
    partitioning **9**
    recovery **11**
distributions **6**
    Debian **19**
    Gentoo **21**
    Knoppix **21**
    RedHat **6**
    SuSE **20**
    Yellow Dog **21**
Domain Name Server **95**, **132**
downloading linux **7**
dual boot **12**
dump **146**

emacs **77**
embedded Linux **199**

emulators
  DOSEMU **89–90**
  VMware **89–90**
  Wine **89, 91**
Ethernet **93**

files
  /etc/exports **110**
  /etc/fstab **38, 162**
  /etc/hosts **95**
  /etc/inetd.conf **120**
  /etc/inittab **172**
  /etc/named.conf **96**
  /etc/passwd **162**
  /etc/resolv.conf **107**
  /etc/syslog.conf **124**
  /etc/xinetd.d/telnet **120**
  /etc/xinetd.d/tftp **128**
  /var/lib/rpm **143**
  /var/log/messages **124**
  hidden **28**
filesystems
  /proc **10, 17, 42**
  ext2 **39**
  ext3 **39**
  HFS **42**
  ISO 9660 **39**
  journalled **177**
  NFS **39, 110**
  recovery **177**
  swap **39**
firewall **135**
fragmentation **94**
Free Software Foundation **4**
fstab **38**

gateway **97**
General Public Licence **4**

hardware requirements **2**
hexadecimal **24**

installation **8**
  text-only **14**
Integrated Development
  Environment **186**
interpreter **184**
  Perl **193**
  TCL **188**

IP address **94**
iptables **135**

kernel **3**
  building modules **203**
  compiling **203**
  configuring **202**
  installing **203**
  patching **205**
kernel parameters **171**

latency **201**
Local Area Network **3**
logging in **25**
loopback **95**

major and minor numbers **43**
man pages **34**
modem **3, 101**
mount point **38**

Network Information Service
  112

online banking **141**
OpenGL **71**

packages
  creating **207**
packet **94**
partitions
  boot **14**
  root **14**
  swap **14**
patents **4**
path
  absolute **28**
  relative **28**
PCI bus **42**
Perl **193**
PostScript **85**
pre-emption **200**
print servers **86**
Printer Control Language **85**
processors
  68000 family **22**
  Alpha **21**
  PowerPC **21**

programs
apmd **17**
automount **112**
bash **77**
convert **65**
cron **81**
DataManager **60**
fdisk **14**, **159**
init **172**
lokkit **135**
lpd **84**
minicom **102**
ODBCConfig **60**
psql **59**
rawrite **9**
tclsh **189**
thttpd **132**
tixwish **189**
wish **189**
protocols
AppleTalk **119**
ARP **100**
CHAP **123**
DecNet **119**
DHCP **100**
FTP **125**
HTTP **95**, **129**
IMAP **74**
NetBIOS extended user
interface (NETBEUI) **114**
NFS **175**
NNTP **75**, **133**
Novell **119**
PAP **123**
PLIP **124**
POP **73**, **74**
PPP **123**
RARP **100**
Server Message Block (SMB)
114
SMTP **73**
TCP **95**
TCP/IP **93**
TFTP **127**
UDP **94**
public key **141**

Qt **187**

real time **200**
recovery
damaged partitions **158**
fsck **159**
GRUB **157**
LILO **158**
Redhat Package Manager
(RPM) **143**
Remote Procedure Call **110**
resolution **107**
RFC **93**
root login **4, 11**
routers **96**
routing table **96**

Samba Web Administration Tool
(SWAT) **115**
Scheifler, Bob **4**
SCSI **43**
Sendmail **73**
serial port parameters **175**
Stallman, Richard **4**
standard input **31**
standard output **31**
SysV init **19, 173**

tab completion **34**
tar **146**
tarball **208**
TCL **188**
text sessions **25**
tix **188**
TK **188**
Torvalds, Linus **4**
training **196**
tux racer **71**

unicode **25**
USB **43**
usenet newsgroups **75, 133**

VAT **8**

widgets **187**

X-Windows
server **43**
window manager **45**

zip **145**

teach
youself

QuarkXPress
christopher lumgair

- Do you need a basic introduction to QuarkXPress?
- Do you want help to create more attractive documents?
- Do you need to brush up your QuarkXPress skills?

QuarkXPress introduces you to the essentials of the program, guiding you through the text entry, page layout and production processes in easy-to-follow stages. By concentrating on techniques, the book will enable you to create well-crafted, professional-looking documents with the minimum of effort.

Christopher Lumgair has a BA in Graphic Design and has spent several years working in both magazine and book publishing. He now runs his own successful digital publishing consultancy.

teach youself

C++
richard riley

- Are you new to programming?
- Do you need to improve your existing C++ skills?
- Do you want to become an expert programmer?

C++ is a concise guide to programming in C++, one of the most popular and versatile languages in use today. All the concepts and techniques you need to create powerful programs are clearly explained, with examples and revision exercises used throughout.

Richard Riley is a computer programmer who has written extensively in C++, Perl, Java, Javascript and HTML.